Creator Suzy Tamasy

EMPOWERED IN HEELS 3

Living with Purpose!

A Collection Of Empowered Stories!

Editor Cathy Simpson

EMPOWERED IN HEELS 3

Amina Bhanji

Judy Swallow

Judy Gaw

Jennifer Middleton

Welcome to a journey of living with purpose and embracing empowerment through Empowered in Heels 3.

In these pages of Empowered in Heels 3 you will discover stories illuminating the extraordinary potential within each of us. These tales are not just stories; they are guiding lights, showing how empowered individuals have harnessed their inner strength to overcome challenges, transform their lives, and leave a positive mark on the world.

From tales of resilience to examples of unwavering determination, Empowered in Heels 3 will introduce you to inspiring individuals who have found their true calling, tapped into their passions, and forged their own unique paths to fulfillment. They are living proof that living with purpose is not a lofty dream but an achievable reality leaving a scent of lavender to inspire you!

Empowered in Heels 3 Living with Purpose, be prepared to be inspired, motivated, and empowered by these stories that will awaken the purpose-driven hero within you. As you turn the pages, let these narratives serve as your mentors, guiding you toward a life filled with meaning, impact, and the unwavering belief that you too can make a difference.

Your journey to living with purpose!

Aceso A

Anju Malhotra

Cathy Simpson

Editor

Suzy Tamasy

Creator

Please check out our other series of Empowered In Heels

1) Empowering you to the next level of Life!
2) Building your Empire!
3) Living with Purpose!

at www.empoweredinheels.org or at Amazon.
Please feel free to leave us a review on Amazon.

If you would like to be part of our next issue please
email us at bizfashion@consultant.com

EMPOWERED IN HEELS Living with Purpose!

Creator Suzy Tamasy

Editor Cathy Simpson

Authors

Aceso A, Amina Bhanji, Jennifer Middleton,

Judy Gaw, Judy Swallow, Anju Malhotra

From our Authors:

"I have never seen myself as an entrepreneur in the traditional sense, nor do feel I have those qualities associated with it but I have to say that I do feel I am an "Entrepreneur of the Soul." Judy Swallow

"Her internal scars heal each day and each day her strong warrior grows". Jennifer Middleton

"Sometimes our darkest moments end up being a blessing in disguise. It's the very pain that pierces through us, that also releases us from bondage".

Amina Bhanji

Table of Content

Suzyqjewels
Women & Children's Program

We are helping hands that reach
out to the lonely and confused.

Together, we can STOP the
cycle of abuse!

98 %

Suzyqjewels Women's & Children's Program has
been helping women and children with counselling,
therapy, shoes for success and legal assistance
since 2000.

20.1 %

Children & Teens
21% of our victims with
counselling and therapy,
social/breaking the cycle go
done.

79.9%

79% of victims are
females. They have
addressed a strong need
for therapy confidence,
independence and
comparable employment.

Together, we can
change lives. Your
help will go a long
way.

Make a donation today
www.suzyqjewels.com

416 262-0816
email:suzyqjewelsWCP@gmail.com
www.SuzyqjewelsWCP.com

Thank you to our Sponsor Publisher Congratulations!

Boss Babe Empowered in Heels!

Photographer Jack Gallagher

Acknowledgement by The Creator

Suzy Tamasy

Welcome to a journey of living with purpose and embracing empowerment through Empowered In Heels 3. In these pages of Empowered In Heels 3 you will discover stories that illuminate the extraordinary potential within each of us. These tales are not just stories; they are guiding lights, showing how ordinary individuals have harnessed their inner strength to overcome challenges, transform their lives, and leave a positive mark on the world.

From tales of resilience to examples of unwavering determination, Empowered In Heels 3 will introduce you to inspiring individuals who have found their true calling, tapped into their passions, and forged their own unique paths to fulfillment. They are living proof that living with purpose is not a lofty dream but an achievable reality leaving a scent of lavender to inspire you!

Empowered In Heels 3 Living with Purpose, be prepared to be inspired, motivated, and empowered by these stories that will awaken the purpose-driven hero within you. As you turn the pages, let these narratives serve as your mentors, guiding you towards a life filled with meaning, impact, and the unwavering belief that you too can make a difference. Your journey to living with purpose leaving you inspired with a scent of lavender through their determination!

Using Your Voice as a Woman

Celebrating the Strength and Diversity of Women

In every corner of the world, women contribute immeasurably to the tapestry of human experience. Their resilience, intelligence, and compassion shape societies, drive progress, and inspire positive change. It's crucial to celebrate the strength and diversity of women, acknowledging the myriad roles they play and the challenges they overcome.

1.   Empowerment Through Education: Women have shown time and again that education is a powerful tool for empowerment. From groundbreaking scientists and engineers to influential leaders and thinkers, women have made significant contributions to every field. Promoting education for girls and women is key to unlocking their full potential and fostering a more inclusive society.

2.	Leadership and Innovation: In the realm of leadership and innovation, women continue to break barriers. From political leaders and CEOs to entrepreneurs and artists, women bring unique perspectives that drive creativity and progress. Recognizing and supporting women in leadership positions not only benefits individuals but also enriches the collective experience.

3.	Strength in Diversity: The strength of women lies in their diversity—diversity of backgrounds, experiences, and perspectives. Women from various cultures, ethnicities, and walks of life contribute to the rich mosaic of human existence. Embracing and celebrating this diversity fosters understanding and promotes a more inclusive and harmonious global community.

4.	Championing Equality: Women have been at the forefront of the fight for gender equality. Their advocacy and activism have led to significant strides in addressing gender-based discrimination and promoting equal opportunities. Recognizing and dismantling barriers that limit the potential of women, benefits not only individuals but society as a whole.

5.	Nurturers and Caregivers: Women have traditionally played crucial roles as nurturers and caregivers.

Their empathy and compassion create strong foundations for families and communities. Valuing and supporting caregiving roles, both within and outside the home, is essential for achieving a balanced and equitable society.

As we celebrate the strength and diversity of women, it is important to recognize the progress that has been made and acknowledge the work that still lies ahead. By championing education, promoting diversity, supporting women in leadership, and advocating for equality, we contribute to a world where the potential of every individual, regardless of gender, can be fully realized. Together, we can build a future where the contributions of women are not only celebrated but also integral to the continued advancement of humanity.

We would like to express our heartfelt gratitude to all the incredible women who have generously shared their powerful and inspiring stories in "Empowered in Heels: Living Through True Stories in Making a Difference to Empower Women." Your courage, resilience, and unwavering commitment to making a positive impact on the world serve as a beacon of hope and inspiration to women everywhere. We extend our deepest appreciation to the countless individuals and organizations that have supported this project along the way. Your belief in the importance of

empowering women and your contributions, whether big or small, have been instrumental in bringing these stories to life. Your commitment to amplifying these voices and stories is commendable.

Lastly, we want to express our gratitude to our readers. Your support and enthusiasm for "Empowered in Heels" drive our mission forward, and we hope that the stories within these pages inspire you to believe in the limitless potential of women and their ability to create meaningful change in the world.

Thank you all for being a part of this empowering journey.

With profound appreciation, Suzy Tamasy

The Stigma of Women Wearing Heels: Empowerment and the Why Behind It

By Suzy Tamasy

High heels have been a staple of women's fashion for centuries, often associated with power, confidence, and elegance. However, the concept of women wearing heels to feel empowered has a complex history and is met with various perspectives. This article explores the stigma surrounding women wearing heels and delves into the reasons why some women choose to do so, shedding light on the deeper motivations beyond mere fashion.

Breaking Down the Stigma

- **Society's Expectations**: One reason for the stigma associated with women wearing heels is rooted in societal expectations. Historically, high heels have been seen as a symbol of femininity and beauty, reinforcing gender norms that dictate how women should present themselves. This pressure to conform to a certain image can make women feel judged or scrutinized when they choose not to wear heels.
- **Physical Discomfort**: High heels are notorious for causing physical discomfort and health issues. Many women who wear heels regularly may face foot pain, back pain, and other related problems. The stigma arises when women are expected to endure this discomfort in the name of empowerment or professionalism.
- **Professional Expectations**: In certain industries, such as fashion, entertainment, or corporate settings, women are often encouraged or even required to wear heels as part of their dress code. This can create a stigma where women feel compelled to wear heels to be taken seriously or advance in their careers.

Why Women Wear Heels for Empowerment

- **Confidence Boost**: For some women, wearing heels provides a confidence boost. The elevated stature and improved posture can make them feel more empowered, assertive, and in control. It's a form of self-expression and personal empowerment.
- **Fashion as Empowerment**: Fashion choices, including wearing heels, can be a way for women to express their individuality and creativity. Empowerment comes from the ability to make choices about one's appearance and style without judgment or constraints.

Cultural Significance: In some cultures, heels have historical or cultural significance as symbols of strength and resilience. Women may choose to wear heels to embrace their cultural heritage and assert their identity.

Breaking Stereotypes: Some women wear heels as a deliberate act of breaking stereotypes. By embracing femininity and wearing heels, they challenge traditional gender roles and expectations, advocating for gender equality on their own terms.

The stigma surrounding women wearing heels to feel empowered is a complex issue deeply ingrained in societal norms and expectations. While high heels can provide a sense of empowerment and confidence to some women, it's essential to recognize that empowerment should not be tied to footwear choices. True empowerment comes from the freedom to express oneself, make choices without judgment, and challenge societal norms and stereotypes.

Ultimately, whether a woman chooses to wear heels or not, her empowerment should be based on her abilities, achievements, and the autonomy to make choices that reflect her values and preferences, rather than conforming to external pressures or expectation.

"Empowered in Heels" and Unpacking the High Heel Stigma: A Comprehensive
Exploration Abstract:

High heels have long been a symbol of femininity, power, and fashion for women. However, beneath the allure and elegance of these shoes lies a complex and often contentious societal stigma. This essay delves deep into both sides of the high heel narrative, exploring the symbolism, history, and societal impact of high heels on women's empowerment, as well as the origins, manifestations, and consequences of the high heel stigma. By examining these facets, we aim to provide a comprehensive understanding of how society views and judges women who wear high heels, shedding light on the complex interplay of fashion, identity, and gender roles. Introduction: Fashion has always been a powerful medium of self-expression, and throughout history, women have used it not only to adorn themselves but also to convey messages of empowerment, confidence, and individuality.

One such avenue where this empowerment is celebrated is through the concept of "Empowered in Heels." This phrase encapsulates the idea that women can feel empowered, confident, and capable of conquering the world while wearing high heels. On the flip side, there exists a societal stigma associated with high heels, often complicating the narrative of empowerment. This essay aims to provide a comprehensive exploration of both aspects, shedding light on the complexities surrounding high heels in modern society.

1. The Symbolism and History of High Heels: High heels have long been regarded as a symbol of femininity, power, and sensuality. They elevate a woman's stature, emphasizing grace and poise. Historically, high heels have been associated with royalty, privilege, and social status, making them a symbol of empowerment in their own right. The act of wearing high heels is akin to putting on a suit of armor for many women, boosting their confidence and self-esteem. High heels have a rich history, evolving from their utilitarian origins to becoming a symbol of status and power.

Understanding this evolution is crucial in comprehending the foundation of the high heel stigma.

1.1. The Height of Confidence: High heels literally elevate women above the ground, changing their posture and gait. This physical transformation often corresponds with a mental transformation, as women feel more confident and assertive when they stand taller. The boost in height and posture helps women command attention and exude self-assuredness. This section can be expanded to explore the psychology of confidence and how it relates to physical appearance.

1.2. Femininity and Sensuality: High heels also play a role in celebrating women's femininity and sensuality. The elongated leg and pointed toe shape created by high heels have been considered attractive and seductive for centuries. Women have embraced this aspect of high heels as a means of self-expression, celebrating their sexuality and embracing their bodies.

Expanding on this, you can discuss how cultural perceptions of femininity have evolved over time and how high heels have adapted to these changes.

2. Historical Evolution of High Heels: The history of high heels is a fascinating journey through time, demonstrating their evolution from a symbol of status to an emblem of empowerment.

2.1. Origins in Ancient Times: High heels have ancient origins, dating back to the Middle East and Persia as early as the 10th century.

These early heels were worn by both men and women and served practical purposes like horseback riding. However, their popularity eventually spread to Europe, where they took on more symbolic meanings. Delve deeper into the cultural exchanges that led to high heels' spread and how their original practicality evolved.

2.2. Royal Symbolism: In Europe, high heels became synonymous with aristocracy and power during the 16th and 17th centuries. European royals, such as Louis XIV of France, were known for their love of high heels, which they wore to assert their dominance and status. The iconic red sole of high heels, now associated with luxury brand, can trace its roots back to this era. Explore the impact of European royal fashion on the broader society and how high heels became aspirational.

2.3. Femininity in the 20th Century: The 20th century saw high heels evolve into a symbol of feminine empowerment. Icons popularized the image of the glamorous, confident woman in high heels. High heels became a staple of women's fashion, embodying both sophistication and strength. Expand on the cultural shifts and women's liberation movements of the 20th century that influenced high heel fashion.

3. Empowerment through Fashion: Fashion has always been a tool for self-expression and empowerment. Women use clothing to convey their identity, values, and aspirations. High heels are just one aspect of this larger narrative.

3.1. Expressing Individuality: Women have diverse reasons for wearing high heels. Some do it for the confidence it imparts, while others view it as a form of self-expression.

Fashion-forward women use high heels to create unique looks and express Empowered in Heels: The concept of "Empowered in Heels" encapsulates the idea that women can feel empowered, confident, and capable of conquering the world while wearing high heels. It's not merely about footwear; it's a symbol of self-assuredness and the celebration of femininity.

3.2.1. The Psychology of Empowerment: Explore in-depth how wearing high heels can trigger a psychological shift in women. The act of putting on high heels can be seen as a form of empowerment. Dive into studies and personal stories that showcase how women feel more in control, assertive, and confident when they wear heels.

2.2. High Heels as a Form of Self-Expression: High heels provide a canvas for self-expression. Women choose from a plethora of styles, colors, and designs, allowing them to tailor their footwear to their personalities and moods. This form of self-expression can be linked to empowerment, as women assert their individuality and break free from societal norms.

3.2.3. Challenging Conventions: Many women have used high heels as a means of challenging conventions. In a world that often dictates how women should look and behave, high heels can symbolize a refusal to conform. Explore stories of women who have used high heels to challenge gender norms and redefine societal expectations.

4. The Ongoing Debate: Despite the celebration of high heels as a symbol of empowerment, there is an ongoing debate surrounding their place in modern society. Critics argue that high heels can be uncomfortable, impractical, and even harmful to women's health.

4.1. Comfort vs. Empowerment: One argument against high heels is that they are not conducive to comfort and mobility. Some women find them painful to wear for extended periods and argue that comfort should not be sacrificed for the sake of empowerment. Explore studies on the physical discomfort caused by high heels and the intersection of comfort and empowerment.

4.2. Health Concerns: There are health concerns associated with wearing high heels regularly. Issues like foot pain, bunions, and back problems have been linked to prolonged high heel use. Critics contend that prioritizing health should outweigh any empowerment gained from wearing high heels. Dive into medical research and expert opinions on the potential health risks of high heels and how these concerns have influenced public perception.

5. The Future of Empowerment in Heels: As society continues to evolve, so does our perception of empowerment through fashion. The future of "Empowered in Heels" lies in embracing diversity, inclusivity, and choice. Women should be free to wear what makes them feel empowered, whether that means high heels, flats, sneakers, or anything in between.

5.1. Choice and Inclusivity: True empowerment comes from having the freedom to choose what one wears without judgment. Society should encourage women to embrace their personal style, whether it involves high heels or not. Inclusivity means recognizing that empowerment can take many forms and should be accessible to all, regardless of gender identity, body shape, or personal preferences. Discuss how fashion industries and brands are evolving to cater to diverse preferences.

5.2. Redefining Beauty Standards: Empowerment in fashion also involves redefining beauty standards. Society is slowly shifting away from narrow definitions of beauty that require women to conform to unrealistic ideals. Empowerment comes from embracing diversity and celebrating individuality. Explore how fashion is evolving to represent a broader range of body types, ethnicities, and identities, and how this contributes to empowerment.

"Empowered in Heels" is a concept that celebrates women's empowerment through fashion and true journey of life, specifically the symbolism and history of high heels. From their origins as symbols of power and status to their evolution into expressions of confidence and sensuality, high heels have played a significant role in women's fashion and empowerment. However, the debate surrounding high heels continues, with critics highlighting issues of comfort and health. The key to the future of empowerment in heels lies in choice, inclusivity, and redefining beauty standards. Women should have the freedom to choose what makes them feel empowered, whether that involves high heels or other forms of self-expression.

Ultimately, empowerment through fashion should be a personal and diverse journey, allowing women to celebrate their individuality and embrace their unique identities.

Whether in heels or any other footwear, women can continue to use fashion as a means of empowerment and self-expression in the ever-evolving world of style. This extended exploration provides a comprehensive view of both the celebration and critique of high heels in contemporary society, shedding light on the multifaceted nature of this intriguing footwear. Cheers to my next chapter of life surprise is on its way!

Giving back to our community with our final bow fashion show showcasing Su-zyqjewels designs on stage at Filafest. Thank you to our lovely models that make me so proud of them that shine lie the Jewels they are!

Miss Heritage 2022 Winners

Miss Heritage Canada 2023

23

Neel Nanda issuing a fashionista award from Heritage Beyond Border to Suzy Tamasy CEO of Bizfashion Media in which she assisted as Judge and Empowerment Coach to the candidates of Miss Heritage Canada 2023 Photocredit by Jonathan Grills

Build your Women Tribe Laugh, Play and Live!

Photography HHMphotography

Models: Moumita, Bree, Rachel, Sumouli,

Fazia, Ebby, Anisha, Helena

Judge for Miss Heritage Canada

**Empowered Sisters Genesis, Shuchi and I
Photographer Jonathan Grills**

Lana & Austyn Polanco June 10 2023 Wedding of my oldest son. He finally ties the knot with his girlfriend over 10 years in which I call my daughter since she lost her loving mother to cancer. Thank you God you always bless us! Just found out I'm going to be a young grandmother at 52 due date June 2024!

Dedication

This book goes out to all the women out there that are superwomen! Thank you to my mother that I call superwomen, sister and my life blessing Austyn & Krystian!

Acknowledgement by our Editor

Cathy Simpson

I'd like to take a moment to thank Suzy Tamasy for giving me the opportunity to be a part of this project. I have edited scripts for movies but never a book. When Suzy approached me to join her team, I was very apprehensive, this was outside of my comfort zone but after becoming a widow I had decided to try anything in order to find my strengths and weaknesses. Well, here was an "anything." Suzy was so engaging and encouraging I felt this was something I wanted to be part of. I have always felt that women should support women, and this was my opportunity to do that.

After reading each story, I came to realize that each and every one of us has a unique perspective of what gave us empowerment. Each of these women experienced a turning point in their lives that lead them to be the women they are today. From trauma to life changing events, there is an opportunity to rise from the ashes. Their courage and strength are overwhelming and inspiring. It shows we can do anything with the right mind set and support. I am extremely honoured to have been entrusted with their stories and given the chance to edit these very personal words.

When my husband had passed away, it left me in a place of self exploration. I had no idea who the real me was. It took me a few years to come to terms with the loss and to find the true me. This loss led me to be the strong resilient woman I am now, who went back to school at 60 years of age and now helps others who suffer from grief to find their strength. All done wearing heels.

It had always been a joke in my life about how high heels were the only thing I could walk in or even run in. My closet holds over 200 pairs of heels, and this is where I often can be found admiring each pair. They are my jewels. After being part of this project, I now look at my heels in a different light. I now realize how I feel when I slip on a pair of heels. My head is held higher, my back is straighter and I'm ready to tackle the world. I too am "Empowered in Heels."

My heartfelt gratitude to Suzy Tamasy for believing in me to help with this project. Also, I'd like to thank all the courageous ladies who had the faith in me to help them express their voice. This has been an amazing experience and one I am thrilled to have participated in.

Finally, to our readers thank you for joining us on our journey to empowerment!

Cathy Simpson

Don't
dream it.
Be it!

Finding Purpose to Pain
By Aceso A

A year ago, I was homeless, suicidal, and jobless. I ran away from home countless times because I was living at home in the room next to my father who sexually assaulted me. My mental health was at its worst and I checked into the emergency room mental health facility and safe houses numerous times. I was a ticking time bomb ready to be gone from this world because I thought dying was the only choice for peace.

A few months later, I moved to downtown Toronto which was my dream place to live. I launched my first business which I co-founded. I got an offer for a job in my dream field, and six months later I got promoted. I worked on myself and found love in a healthy, and stable relationship. I signed a book offer and I am writing my story on a train in Europe. You may think a miracle happened to completely turn my life around from being suicidal to happy, in less than a year. A miracle did not happen, it was all possible due to the skills and lessons that I learned that got me here, all of which I will share in this chapter to hopefully inspire you.

Everyone has trauma, I certainly did, a lot of it. Most people let trauma consume them which makes people lose control over their life. What if I told you, you could use your trauma to find your deepest truths, and purpose to create passion, fulfillment, and joy, if used correctly?

In this chapter, I will be sharing my journey of everything that I learned to not only cope with trauma but to utilize my trauma to serve me and turn my life completely around in less than a year. I will be sharing my childhood trauma, and how I finally chose myself by changing my mindset to turn my dream turned into reality.

The first step is wanting to be happy; the second step is creating a happy life. Most people struggle with the second step because they are stuck in a negative mindset that formed during childhood in a toxic environment. Most people do not know how to change their thoughts that were developed through trauma, abuse, and or neglect I hope my story will inspire you to make your trauma serve you, rather than serving your trauma.

I was molested by my father at ten years old. I woke up with his hands in my vagina and touching my breasts. I acted like nothing was wrong. My coping mechanism for the next decade was denial. My inner thoughts were not negative about the situation, and I moved on as if nothing happened. My home life was already so chaotic, and I never expressed the amount of stress I had. I already had so much stress that I could not add more trauma. If I confronted my true feelings about the event, I would have certainly broken down.

By age ten I was raising my younger brother and working in my family business I was changing and feeding my brother because my parents were working and did not have time. My schedule after school every day and on weekends would be tailored around my brother. My parents were industrious immigrants who worked a lot to build everything they had. I had to attend appointments, meetings, and phone calls for the business. By age eleven, I helped my parents buy their first property. I remember being so stressed about my first landlord-tenant board hearing to evict a tenant. Little me was the head of the household by age twelve. I helped make a lot of decisions in real estate, investing, business, and as a landlord. I remember real estate agents would eventually turn to me to ask if I wanted to buy the property since my mom trusted me for investments. I developed an excellent sense of investing, problem-solving, and communication skills. I had looked at many properties. I understood the key factors for successful investment properties which were location, timing of the economy, price, and quality. In addition to managing a lot of backend work, I spent a lot of time in their businesses such as taking orders, waitressing, and as a cashier, especially on weekends.

On top of the immense number of responsibilities, I was living in trauma and a large amount of stress for my entire childhood. I never talked back to my parents, especially my mom. I endured screaming fits and hitting by agreeing that I was stupid, and worthless in order to calm them down. No matter how busy I was, I would always complete the tasks I was asked to do. For example, I had school, my brother to raise, taxes to do, CRA and banks to call, bank appointments, work, the house to clean, grass and insurance companies to call all in a few days at twelve years old. Of course, I was tired, and I did not want to do it. I felt like I had to, I could not say no, and I was terrified to say no. I gave up my entire childhood. In return, I never asked for a single thing. I remember there was a school ski trip when I was thirteen. It was 500 dollars, and I was one of the few students who did not go. Not because my parents did not have money, they did. I could not choose myself, despite all the efforts I dedicated to helping my parents. I survived by burying what my father did to me. I could not have handled my entire reality; I chose to swim instead of sink. My relationship with my dad remained the same. He would drive me to places, we had simple conversations about life.

When I was eighteen years old, I moved out of home and into the dorms of my university. It was the happiest year of my life. I finally experienced freedom and a balanced healthy life. For the first time, I was prioritizing myself and what I wanted, at least from Monday to Friday. For a year, I was not under immense stress from my family. My mom would still call me every Friday night and make me come home for the weekend I would wake up at nine every Saturday morning and take the bus to go home because I did not have the guts to tell her how I truly felt, I did not want to go home. I was eating better since I had a meal card to buy food, instead of starving at home and eating frozen meals. I could go to class, study, and have fun with my friends and prioritize myself. I lived my age for the first time in my life. This changed my life because I realized what kind of life other people were living, what "normal" was without immense amounts of pressure, responsibility, and chaos.

After my first year of university, I moved home since my parents lived in the same city as my university. After tasting a life where I was the main priority of my life, I fell into a deep depression when I had to go back home. I had no idea what depression felt like and what mental health even meant. The only emotions I felt were sadness, confusion, and hopelessness. I knew I could not move back home. I needed my parents' help financially to let me live in student housing. I spent my whole childhood serving my parents by raising their son, building their business, and working in their business, heck I even did their taxes but when I asked them for a ride to dinner with my friends, it was a no. I knew this was going to be extremely difficult or impossible. My only way was to tell them I wanted to live out of their house because I was depressed, but Asian parents do not know what mental health or depression is. Some of them do not even believe in it. I had never even talked to them about it.

I remember so distinctly; I mustered enough courage to tell my mom I had depression and had to move out. Her response was "If you move out, I will get depression." My dad's response was "Do you think moving out will fix your depression? It is not going to work." Rent at that point was around four hundred dollars a month. I would never ask for that much unless it was really important to me. My dream at that point was to be a physician because at sixteen years old I decided that my purpose was to make the biggest impact possible and that was through healthcare. Medical school in Canada was extremely hard to get into. My grades had to be perfect. Growing up, I learned to study hard. In university I had to study hard, more than I had before, which was a lot, and it still was not enough. This meant I could not maintain a good GPA during the school year on top of work. I already did poorly in a few classes in my first year and I needed perfection from then on. I had to choose between working to financially support myself to pay rent or doing well in school. I chose to do well in school. I worked that summer for my mom however, it was not enough. I needed my parent's financial help.

Summer of 2019, I was studying for the MCAT, the medical school entrance exam, and working for my mom. My relationship with her got worse. I was severely suicidal at this point and prayed for God to let me go. Every day felt like another lifetime and the goal was to keep myself alive and not kill myself. I was a ticking time bomb. I started seeing the family doctor on campus who was my savior during this time. She booked me appointments with her three times a week because I think she was worried about my safety. This one weekend in August, she asked me if I would hurt myself because I was going home to work for my mom. I was honest and was not sure if I would be alive past the weekend. The amount of pain I was in consumed me, it made me drink, and cut myself. This was the first time I ever cut myself and I never understood why people would do that until then. The mental pain was so bad, and I wanted any kind of distraction to release pain which was cutting my wrists. I knew this weekend would be bad because I had just admitted to being depressed, and that I felt I needed to move out to be alive. My counselor and everyone told me I had to say it out loud, so I did. The feeling was that my family did everything for me and were offended that I would blame anyone.

That Friday when I arrived for work, the family went on a rampage saying how they immigrated to Canada for me, they sent me to Europe for vacation, and they gave up so much for me. I broke into a panic attack and was bawling my eyes out in the washroom while rocking myself back and forth repeating: "I want to die". They did not know how to respond, and I told them to go home, and they did. I was the only person working that night. I worked the night shift on Friday nights from six p.m. to two a.m., in a dangerous neighbourhood. I was confused as to why my family would even put me in this situation. I had to pull myself together to take orders and make sandwiches for customers, and I had no idea how I was going to do that. I remember I was still crying profusely as I made a customer's sandwich and I thought to myself "God please help me." The next customer who walked in asked me if I was okay. I said, "No, I am having a mental breakdown." She said, "I am a psychiatric nurse, and I am going to help you." The nurse convinced me to go to the emergency room at the hospital and called my dad to take over my shift. I remember the look on my dad and brother's faces so vividly. They were shocked, concerned, and sad for me all at the same time. The nurse drove me to the ER and said she never goes to the restaurant that late. However, she had a sudden feeling that she needed to go and get a sandwich. Her husband called her and said he wanted food from there too. She said it was so strange and she felt like she was sup-posed to be there to help me. She asked me about my situation and asked me what I was living for. I said I am living to make an impact to help people, through the deepest means possible which was through health care. She went on a motivational speech saying I needed to stay alive for the people I will heal. I added the nurse on Facebook and thanked her for saving me. I still keep in touch with her today. She dropped me off and I waited in the emergency room for seven hours. By the
time I saw the physician, I felt a lot better. The physician knew my family doctor at the university and trusted that I would not hurt myself. They called me a taxi home at six in the morning.

Initially, I was quiet in the taxi and just reflecting on what had happened. The taxi driver asked me what was wrong. I was hesitant but he seemed caring and wanted to know. I told him I went to the emergency room because I was feeling suicidal. He started a conversation and asked me what made me want to live. I said to heal people and my brother. He said, "I lost my own brother to suicide because of mental health. It caused so much sadness in me, that I even con-sidered ending my own life. If you love your brother, do not do that. You are given a gift to heal people and you will not stop your life here. If you need someone to talk to, call me. If you need somewhere to go, I will take you." His story touched the depths of my broken soul and healed some cracks. I realized I had only been thinking about my own pain. My life could be so much worse, I could not lose myself and hurt my brother no matter how much pain I was in. This event made me not suicidal anymore. For the rest of my life, killing myself was not an option. It took so much for me to realize this, but I sincerely think God sent angels, the nurse and the taxi driver into my life to help me. He did not want me to go. No matter how much I begged and tried, God saved me. I asked for help, and he gave it to me. It was time to accept life, instead of fighting it. I did not know how I was going to accept life, but I was going to do it.

Father Issues

I did not realize I was sexually assaulted by my father until almost 10 years later when I turned twenty-two years old. That was when the Jeffrey Epstein case was everywhere, and I was really invested in reading about the terrible abuse he had done to underage girls. That is when it hit me and everything clicked as if my entire life shattered, my dad molested me. My first thought was I saw so many sexual assault stories and the victim was confused about what had happened. I always thought it was strange how one could not realize what had happened until years later and yet I was the one going through the same thing. My second thought was "How could my dad be so stupid that he did not know what he did to me, that it was wrong?" My mom was always the brains of the family, who delegated what to do. She had always complained about how my dad did not think and was careless. She was right. My dad did not have financial plans, did not really care much about his children, and preferred to be on the computer rather than spending time with people. I remember sleeping on a wooden bed frame instead of a mattress. I would constantly ask him for a mattress since it was so hard to sleep on and he would keep on saying "Later". It was not until a friend's mom felt bad and gave me a bed. Even when we did not have toilet paper or other simple necessities, he would rather be on his computer for twenty-four hours a day than go to the store which was five minutes away. It made sense why I thought he never thought about the impact of what he had done, he was self-consumed and negligent.

Conveniently, this was during quarantine which allowed me to have the time to think about absolutely everything wrong with my life. I broke down every day about my trauma from my father, on top of my existing childhood trauma. This was one of the hardest times in my life. I knew parenting was hard, but was it this hard? Is it so hard to not abuse your kids? Is it so hard to not sexually abuse your kids? The biggest pain was being let down by both of my parents so badly that I developed PTSD. It was a coin toss every day if I was going to be angry and depressed about my mom or dad. The worst part of all was that my brother is the person I love the most in the world and he was being parented by the people who hurt me the most. I lived in extreme anxiety, depression, anger, and pain. On top of that, I was finishing up my last year of university and quarantined at home with nowhere to go. I only had my deep dark thoughts to haunt me. My brain was like a television, replaying every scene of abuse as if it was happening again, without stopping.

Business

Amongst all the chaos, I had this intense burning desire to start a business. It began when I was sitting in my room during COVID and simply googled "bubble tea t-shirt". As an avid fanatic of bubble tea, I figured there had to be a shirt with a bubble tea design. To my surprise, all the designs were atrocious. They either had huge bubble tea designs with neon colours, googly eyes, or weird slogans. I went through every page on Google search, shopping, and images and found no design that I would actually buy. This puzzled me as bubble tea is a huge phenomenon enjoyed by all races, genders, and ages. There are bubble tea stores everywhere, memes about bubble tea, and bubble tea merchandise like lamps, and plushies. Enjoying bubble tea has become a social activity people do on dates, with friends, with family, and as a treat for themselves. I wondered, "Why is there not a single bubble tea t-shirt design that I or anyone that I know would buy?" This stimulated an intense drive to start my own company making bubble tea t-shirts. I knew if I did not do it, someone else would, and I could not let that happen.

All those years of helping my mother with her businesses and investing in real estate made me into a strong businesswoman. I saw a business opportunity and I took action to make an idea into reality despite my circumstances and age. Formulating a business idea is not the hard part. Acting on it is where most people stop. My mother forced me to take action for her businesses and she took many risks which I call "good risks". Good risks are calculated to work in my favour if executed properly. I knew I already possessed at least the basic backbone skills to become an entrepreneur. I had enough guts to turn an idea into reality which is because my mom threw me into the business world since I was ten years old. She relied on me to build her businesses which in return taught me how to develop an idea worth investing, problem solve any issues that arose, and trust me there were a lot. I wanted to become a successful entrepreneur, but I knew it would take time to make money. I had that patience because I trusted the skills, I had because of what I went through. I knew the only way to become a successful entrepreneur was to do it.

So, I did. I realized there was a huge demand for bubble tea including its merchandise but no supply. I researched every day coming up with ideas, and business plans and I could not let it go, so I decided to do it. I told my best friend about the idea who studied business and she became my co-founder. Soon enough, I worked with my friend in graphic design to come up with designs. We spent months brainstorming, designing, and re-designing. We created surveys for all of our close friends to choose which designs they liked best to generate research and data. After that, we found an Ontario-based manufacturer who worked with the Gap, OVO, and Youtuber Pewdiepie. Every dot we created was strategized, researched, and thought through. There were seven-hour meetings three times a week on top of our full-time jobs, and I did this all while in my college room, then couch-crashing at my friend's places. I was so obsessed with working on Oppa's Closet, that it became my firstborn child. I created it with my two hands. It was the best distraction from my chaotic personal life. It was hard at times to be so busy, but I loved it.

I always wished I lived a normal childhood. I was depended on so much that I envied the other children who did not have to have responsibilities like an adult. However, twelve years later, all of those responsibilities allowed me to launch my first business from scratch and know in the depths of my soul that I am made to be a successful entrepreneur and I will. My childhood allowed me to develop and hone skills to be an entrepreneur for more than a decade already, which other people do not have. I could sulk about how my parents relied on me or I could use all the skills I developed to become a successful businesswoman. I chose the latter and this is what made me start Oppa's Closet at twenty-two years old, in my college bedroom.

The lowest point was my turning point to my highest point.

Fast forward a few months later, I had to move back home because I finished my university studies and had no money to move out again. I had to live beside my father whose bedroom was right next to mine. This broke me and I ran away from home every day. I would sleep on my friend's couches, and even stay over at my friend's dad's girlfriend's. I was at the peak of survival mode, and I had no idea what to do. I had to get a job to move out, and I applied for months but no response. I was in so much pain every day that it became very difficult to apply for jobs. The basic foundation of my life, safety, was not met so it was challenging to do work. It was the dead of winter and I escaped to the baseball field near my house to smoke weed because I just wanted to turn my brain off. I was trapped in my own mind. Although I was not suicidal anymore, I felt the same amount of pain. Before, I was suicidal because I felt like there was no way out except to commit suicide. As bad as it sounds, thinking of committing suicide allowed me to release my pain onto an idea that I thought would solve my problems. I do not recommend this at all, and this is completely false. The right mindset is "Everything is solvable" and "How do I fix this?" which I learned later.

This time, I wanted to live but I was not living. I had no way to release my energy, so I turned to substance use every day. Before I even realized it, I developed a terrible addiction. I was stuck and I could not get myself out. I knew I needed help, so I contacted my physician who helped me in the past. She connected me with the Youth Addictions program at my local hospital. They had psychiatrists who could help me reanalyze my medication and re-evaluate my diagnosis. I started seeing an addictions counselor. I knew I needed a trauma counselor because the root cause of my addictions was my trauma. However, they were expensive, and I was an unemployed new graduate. I kept on running away from home and soon enough I broke down and had a panic attack. I called the police to help me and I was sent to a safe house.

Life Started When I Chose Myself

My psychiatrist advised me years ago to "play dead" when something bothered me to protect my peace. In one ear and out the other ear. This was nearly impossible being around a toxic environment. A year later I moved to downtown Toronto which was my dream city to live in Canada, and I finally protected my peace. I realized a lot of my happiness depended on my environment, so I needed to move. I was done surviving, I wanted to be in an environment that made me the happiest which was Toronto. I could not be in the suburbs anymore because that could risk further unhappiness. A friend at the time was looking for a new roommate. I finally mustered up enough courage to move, to choose myself. I asked my mom to help me pay the first and last rent because I was no longer going to feel bad for asking. In order to be happy, I had to demand happiness from myself and other people who could help me. No more compensating my own happiness for other people and it worked.

In the month of May, I took a job waitressing to save up money, and I launched my first company, Oppa's Closet. By July, I moved to downtown Toronto. I did not have enough money saved up for the remaining months, but I did everything I could to make ends meet. My environment was no longer toxic, I was living in my dream city, and this made me want to work relentlessly to stay happy.

The reason why I was scared of choosing myself is because I was scared to fail. I did not fail. There was nothing left in my cup, so I chose another cup.

I worked at a retail store in Eaton Centre while still applying for jobs in mental health. I got a job as a Support Worker which they gave me during the interview. I showered, changed, and cleaned poop for the elderly. I never once resented my job or thought I was overqualified as a graduate with a Bachelor's in Science. I was grateful to be there, and I took every job I could to make ends meet. On top of that, I was tutoring chemistry. I worked three jobs on top of running my own company, working almost a hundred hours a week, seven days a week to stay in Toronto. I was on fire. The drive and motivation all came out because I finally lived in peace. Soon enough I got a call to do an interview for Salvation Army as a Day Program Counsellor to help clients with autism spectrum disorder, developmental disorders, depression, anxiety, and schizophrenia. It was the first interview I received after being unemployed for so long and I got the job. I worked hard and was promoted to primary case worker after six months. I loved my job and clients, one of them even emailed my manager applauding my skill set within a few months of my job. I went to New York City to visit Columbia University and New York University to gain motivation for my Master of Counseling programs. I became happier than ever; I was stable and my relationship with my mom was better than ever. She called me frequently to chat about life and even gossip as if we were friends and we did become friends. I went from being in so much pain from my parents to forgiving my parents to appreciating my parents, at least my mom. I was able to be at the same table as my father for the holidays. This all happened because I chose myself, I figured out a plan that would make me the happiest and I just did it. Creating a distance from my family allowed me to love them more. The distance allowed me to experience the positives from my parents and not the negatives. If it got too much, I had the option to go to my own safe place.

People are in your life for a few seasons. Even your own blood. It is okay to step away from your family, only then can you and your relationship bloom.

I no longer gave myself excuses that stopped me from being happy. For years my excuses were "I am still young, I do not have money, I cannot afford it, I should wait until I pay off my student debt and I will just wait until I find a full-time job in the city." The most ideal, logical plan would be to wait until I find a stable full-time job in the city, save up enough money to ensure I can pay rent, so I do not have so much financial pressure, and then move. I tried that and it did not work. I could have blamed my situation on COVID, being a new graduate, or my parents for making me feel miserable but that meant I would have stayed in a toxic environment longer. I was not going to do that anymore, I wanted to choose myself. I was not going to wait around for the job market to choose me anymore, I was not going to wait for the world to choose me anymore, I was going to choose myself by figuring out what made me happy and doing it. No more excuses, only how. Looking back, I learned the pain I felt was the world wanting me to change my situation. The more I remained in a toxic environment, the worse it got, the world pushed me harder, and my mental health became worse. Now that I am living my dream life, I can appreciate everything I experienced. I can say my life is worth it, all the tears were worth it. When life feels miserable, I encourage you to start choosing yourself to make a change in your life, no matter how difficult or impossible it feels. God, or the universe, whichever you believe, is telling you something. You have to listen and choose yourself. After you choose yourself, the world chooses you. I chose myself and then the world gave me everything that I wanted. I had to learn how to fight for my happiness first, in order to get my dream job, get promoted, live in my dream city, find love, and achieve more than I could ever dreamed of. The first step was always me.

The strongest people are the ones who are still kind to themselves, even when life tore them apart.

How I healed:

Purpose

I run on purpose. When I felt like I had no reason to live, I constantly reminded myself of my purpose in life. Why I was living, what I was doing all of this for. When I was fifteen years old, I knew I wanted to make an impact. At the end of my life on my deathbed, I wanted to feel like I helped as many people as possible. I thought about the deepest way I could make an impact. I knew people lived to be happy, make money, make memories, and create life. None of this can be obtained if people are not alive or are not healthy. I realized my purpose was to help people be alive. I wanted to be a doctor. I dedicated my teenage years to achieving the highest possible grades and extraordinary extracurriculars to get into a good university program and then medical school. I wrote the seven-hour medical school entrance exam, MCAT, did research, was president of the STEM Fellowship club, was a member of Junior Team Canada representing my city, and many more. I even took a fifth year of university to finish my American medical school course requirements, just in case. Everything I thought I knew became confusing and I needed to reanalyze everything. I call this the "post-graduate depression" which was when my life goals were really re-analyzed. I figured out what kind of lifestyle I wanted, before what kind of job I wanted. This led me to realize I wanted to never work a day in my life on top of loving my job.

As a child of immigrant parents, I saw how my parents worked jobs they did not like to support the family financially. I learned from their excellent work ethic. In my mind, their sacrifice was worth it if I worked in a job that I loved and also made money. I developed a burning desire to find that career path. This was definitely not medicine as physicians dedicate majority of their lives to their jobs. I wanted to be an entrepreneur, have a full-time job in healthcare, spend time with my children, and have leisure time to have fun and experience the world. I knew it was hard to have it all, but I wanted to at least try to have it all. Being a physician would not allow me to do that and it would set me up for a life that I did not want, although it satisfied my purpose.

I realized I was listening to a lot of my friend's problems and worries and making them feel better. In fact, I was doing this for friends, family, family friends, mutual friends, and people whom I did not even know. I loved psychoanalyzing words, behaviours, and body language, and I realized that my analyses were usually right. I loved figuring out people's root problems and identifying the source of their misery. People felt like I understood them without them clearly understanding themselves. I was putting feelings into words, and words into comfort, and comfort into actions to help people. My words made an impact on people and I was good at it.

My words became my superpower. I found my superpower through my trauma.

The feeling when my own words pulled people out of panic attacks and helped them feel less anxious, depressed, and more at ease was incredible.

People trusted me with their deepest problems and to make me feel better. This was the best eureka moment of my life. Months of being confused, and stressed, while battling PTSD from my childhood traumas led to this moment. I felt like I could feel one's emotions and help people in pain because of my own mental health struggles. Compassion is to suffer together, and empathy is to feel one's emotions, both of which are the basic foundational skills for thera-pists. My superpower of healing people would not be possible without my own suffering. Each time I helped someone, especially those with childhood trauma and sexual assault, made me feel like my own childhood traumas and sexual assault were worth it as weird as it sounds. I could use my own pain, and how I healed myself to help countless other people. I felt like being a psychotherapist was at the same time my saviour, purpose, and calling. This made me want to live and remind myself that I have so many people in the world to save if I could just continue to save myself.

My first job was as a Community Mental Health Worker for convicted felons who plead not guilty, due to mental health. My clients had a combination of dif-ferent mental health diagnoses, most commonly schizophrenia. I came to work with a gentleman who due to his trauma, found himself admitted to the facility where I worked. He had been accused of a terrible crime, which came about, due to his hallucinations. His mental health issues lead him to be admitted to several facilities over the course of twenty years. While working with him, he struggled coming to terms with what had happened and experienced much confusion, sadness and pain, even though it had been decades. I was still liv-ing in the same house as my father at the time and it was the first Fathers Day after realizing he had molested me. I had a shift on Father's Day, I went to work, and I saw him staring into space on the patio and immediately talked to him. He was in tears of regret and remorse. I talked to him to support him, and we developed a professional bond where he trusted me and I made him feel better. He did not even have to thank me since it was my job but seeing his emotions stabilize filled my soul with the utmost happiness and soothed my own childhood wounds.

I realized I spent most of my life surrounded by people who lived simple lives compared to my clients. The bubble that I created was the reality of my own world when in reality, there are people who are suffering a lot more than me, who are still doing their best to live and are still kind. I always knew people had it worse, but it was at that moment when I experienced it myself and saw it with my own eyes. This experience made me thankful for my own past as painful as it was because it gave me the ability to make people feel better. I was going to utilize this and help as many people as I can. I was not going to let myself be traumatized anymore, I was going to make a net positive by helping people and healing myself too. Find your purpose that is true to you, that makes you enjoy life, and remind yourself every day of why you are here and look back to it when you are questioning life. It needs to be strong enough to keep you from sinking. My childhood trauma of struggling with mental health, surviving sexual assault, and having my childhood stripped from me, abuse, and neglect allowed me to develop my superpower of healing people's mental health. I am lucky enough to have my purpose be my full-time job which I can practice five days a week and help people, which gives me the greatest gratitude and appreciation for life. I could have suffered and developed those skills to be a counselor but not utilized them to their maximum potential. I could have not suffered but perhaps worked a job that generated money, which was what I prayed for so long but because I utilized my trauma, and developed positive traits despite my trauma, I am living my dream life. Both scenarios are acceptable, and many people live through those scenarios. However, I like my life better.

Life Mottos that I Live By that Made Me Turn My Pain into Success. Learn from the best, avoid the bad

The more I grow up, the more I realize humans take after their parents' traits, the good and bad and it is very difficult to control which traits to take after unless you make a diligent effort to be self-aware and change. Whether I liked my parents or not, they are my main examples of how to communicate, behave, love, and live. I made it my life goal to not replicate my parent's negative behaviors. For every argument, dispute, or issue I have, I always see how I could have improved. I try to look at people's perspectives and see what I did wrong. In my opinion, arguments with people I care about are a gold mine for self-improvement. If I do not improve myself, the problem will continuously arise until I improve.

My biggest accomplishment is healing from my trauma, so I do not become the very people who hurt me. That is priceless.

I realized most people fight because they think they are right which makes people stay the same and I strongly believe this is setting people up for failure and miserable lives. Even if someone has made them upset if I deny my own contributions to the negative outcome, I will continuously experience the same problem with someone else, somewhere else. When I have a problem, the problem is not the other person, the problem is the situation. Putting blame on the world, or someone else does nothing for me, except make my insecurity happy and my ego soar. I am twenty-five years old; I cannot act like I am perfect. I do not believe there is any age or point where I will not have anything to improve. I will never be perfect, but I can be fantastic.

I am constantly improving which allows me to gain positive traits, build a better mindset, be a better person, and reach bigger success. How do you evolve if you think you are perfect? I realized most of the population does not do this. People choose what to see and improve on which makes them stuck in the mentality of a child forever. The only person hurt in the end by this mentality is themselves. I understand everyone is insecure, whether about external or internal aspects of themselves. No matter how insecure I am, I will always take every situation and problem to improve myself because that is how I value myself.

If person A can improve themselves for the rest of their life, and person B cannot improve because they are insecure and would never allow themselves to think badly, guess who will be happier and more successful?

Not only do I seek to continuously improve my mentality, but I also improve my personal skills. For example, before I could not cook. I watched videos on cooking and became a good cook. Instead of saying "I cannot cook", I ask myself "How can I be a good cook?" I was not good at putting on makeup, but I learned how-to put-on makeup and made myself look more put together. I had a fight with a friend who said I was too blunt, and it was hurtful. Instead of blaming her for being too sensitive, I considered it and watched my words more, especially when I spoke to her. Other friends after her have brought up that I am blunt, even though I was trying to improve. I know I cannot change overnight but I am getting better. Had I dismissed all of my friends and blamed them for being sensitive then I would probably have fewer friends and be blunt for the rest of my life.

I learned to look up to those around me who have traits that are better than me. I am not jealous because that leads to thoughts of "I cannot be better." I learn from those I admire and replicate. I understand there are traits from people I admire that I cannot replicate, like physical looks. I realized there will always be someone better looking than me, skinnier than me, taller than me, and the list is endless. When I am skinny, I wish I had more curves to look sexier. I cannot and will not ever win. Therefore, the only way to win with physical looks is to not play the game at all. I exercise to be healthy; I have a good skincare routine to fix acne, I put on makeup and hair to look better and that is it. The only way to win in the game of beauty is to try my best with what I have and then not play at all.

We are made on this earth to experience life and people. Every experience, the good and the bad, but especially the bad tells you something. I have turned my life around immensely by looking into ways to improve in every situation. I dedicate most of my successes, in my career, and in my personal life like having such an amazing support system and developing healthy loving relationships to this one mentality of persistent and continuous improvement. Be secure enough to be wrong. Be confident enough to improve. Love yourself enough, the right way, and evolve forever.

Forgiveness

You have probably heard this before, forgive them for yourself, not them. I did not understand the power of this until heartbreak. I was severely impacted by breakups, more than most people. This was because of my issues with my father. My trauma stopped me from trusting men, and I stopped trusting men. My heart built ten-foot walls and I would only bring them down for the right man. Once I found a man who I thought would meet my criteria, I fell deep and fast, without my own control, my heart sang to their heartbeat, and I danced to their rhythm. When it did not work out, I felt like my heart shattered into pieces and I was physically picking up every piece and stapling it back up again. Every piece of advice I found told me only time and focusing on myself could make me feel better. I could not control time. Working on my career, working out, and spending time with friends were all distractions from my root problem, which was the heartbreak. Each heartbreak brought so much excruciating pain which was a part of the reason why I was alone for so long.

The most recent heartbreak I discovered something that changed my life. I forgave him. Time heals because it blurs all the emotions and feelings attached to the relationship and person. Unfortunately, no one can control time.

The right mindset propels you to your future self who is healed.

I jumped to my higher future self who was able to move on and love again, by forgiving my partner, even though he made mistakes. I did it for him, but largely for myself and my future husband. I was not going to let my father, or any other man who did me wrong dictate my life to be alone anymore. I took back control of my life by forgiving him. A lot of the time, heartbreak hurts because we are thinking about how we were treated wrong and missing them. The person becomes a drug that we are addicted to, and the breakup becomes withdrawal. Once I forgave him, all of the pain went away, as if the scars from my heart were lifted and left my body entirely.

If you cannot forgive your abuser, forgive them for yourself and walk away to choose better. Mindset dictates your actions and actions dictate your future. Even if you move on from your abuser, your mind might still long for him, and your reality is still cycling through the same mistakes. Step into your higher power for yourself.

How I Became Successful Despite Trauma

Battling My Root Cause

Children who have experienced trauma often have a skewed perspective of themselves. A generalized model I use to help analyze this is by looking at the two extremes of unhealthy self-esteem and their lifelong effects.

On one hand, children who were victims of trauma may overcompensate for their neglect and lack of affection by becoming egotistical. They might try to build an image of themselves that is powerful and indestructible. Children need at least some amount of love, positive affirmations, and reassurance to build self-esteem. When children lack these necessities to build a healthy esteem, become very insecure and build an esteem themselves that becomes unreasonably high to overcompensate their toxic environment. They grow an internal voice of validation to survive. The people in their environment might talk down on them, but they tell themselves they are amazing in order to cope. This leads to developing an unreasonably high sense of importance, which leads to the narrative that everyone else is flawed and to blame every factor but themselves. The worst thing you can say to these people is that they are wrong or not good enough because this is the root of the initial problem. This attacks their esteem, and their wall will be higher than ever to protect. They will choose themselves before everyone else and this may be viewed as selfish which in a way it is but shielding unfavourable language and reaffirm positive language to themselves.

This of course leads to problems for growth and improvement. My biggest advice to these types of people is to confront the root problem that led them to think this way. Who caused this? What caused this? Most likely this happened during childhood, and I advise them to heal their inner childhood wound properly which will allow the wall to break down. To convince this type of person to be better is to encourage that improvement and change is for them.

I realized this and understood my mom so much more. Being my mom's child, I cannot change her but only understand and distance myself when it gets too much. It took years to develop the courage to choose myself and to not be in that environment and it empowered me to live my own life.

The other outcome for children of trauma is self-hatred, thinking they are not good enough and they are the problem when it is not. Both examples faced criticism and perhaps abuse. This type listened and believed their abuser, and this ruined their esteem, but they never built an inner voice to compensate for the lack of affection. They will feel bad for situations that are not their fault and usually place someone else's happiness and needs above their own because that is how they handle problems. They are likely to be dependent on others for validation and often find themselves stuck in relationships with abusive and narcissistic partners. They might feel like they do not deserve happiness and are likely to be stuck in situations where they give to other people way too much. My biggest advice is to take action to be out of the toxic environment that caused this. Staying will only continue this kind of behavior. Then, to do a lot of self-affirmations, and therapy to grow and build an esteem. Constant reminders they are worthy of happiness, love, and success. These types of people usually struggle with this and are scared to develop a high ego. Depending on the severity of their insecurities, this is not likely.

I am this example. For years, I was pouring love for other people, more than I had, which led me to be empty. That allows me to care and empathize with people. That is an amazing trait. However, because I can do this, I am more than deserving to live a happy life and think highly of myself. I need to pull myself to a midline of self-esteem. Not too much where I am the first outcome and cannot grow but not overcompensating for other people anymore. When people compliment me, I can listen and take in what they are saying and not brush it off and go back to my self-loathing monologue.

Self-loathing		Bal-
ance	Self-idolatry	
Outcome 2		Healthy Mind-
set	Outcome 1	

Everything in life follows balance. Too much of anything is problematic, too little of anything is problematic. I had to pull myself to the middle, to build esteem in order to choose myself and live how I am supposed to live. I made this a priority. If I can study hours a day and work eight hours a day, then I can work on myself. I believe society prioritizes people to work on the external aspects a lot more than internal which is why so many people are unhappy and struggling. Generally, we go to school for six hours a day to work forty hours a week to make money. We buy products and, work out to look better. We work to buy cars, homes, more stuff, and vacations and none of this truly improves our internal self. Vacations can help us release stress and reset our minds. Buying stuff, we want can help us feel like we achieved a goal and are worthy. None of this actually fixes our root problems and everyone has them. Every bad habit stems from unresolved trauma. Nothing in society teaches us to actually improve our mindset and trauma. We need to choose and learn how to. That is why therapy is a booming industry now. People are realizing money does not create long-term happiness if our internal self is struggling. I refused to work so hard and not be happy at the end of my life. That is why I make an effort to improve my internal self as much as I work.

I sought out therapy when I was nineteen years old when I realized something was deeply wrong. I got diagnosed and re-diagnosed by five psychiatrists to determine what I have and to be on the right medication to help my serotonin levels while I attended therapy. I participated in eight months of intensive diabolical behavioral therapy to fix my trauma from my dad and improve my outlook on men. I went to trauma therapy to understand and relieve the pain from my childhood. I journal and watch videos on self-love, and mental health, and read about trauma consistently. Most importantly, I wanted to live better, change and improve. I took action to do so and made it such a priority that it was like preparing for war. I had the best friends who were always there for me, and I learned how to support myself. I saw it as a battle because I was destroying myself. I build a fort by moving out of my parent's home and moving to my dream place. I bought all my weapons by taking therapy seriously, doing my homework, and reading to change my brain pathways to a healthy mindset.

I allocated my troops by surrounding myself with caring, kind friends who supported my mental health and rooted for happiness. I trained myself by living a healthy lifestyle by meal prepping home-cooked healthy meals, working out, ensuring my space is clean, and most importantly training my brain to snap out of negative thoughts when they were not real. The last one is the most difficult which took a lot of therapy and practice. I wanted to hate every man who even looked at me. Instead of being disgusted and thinking, every man wants to hurt me, I had to snap out of it and be logical. Is that man actually degrading me or is he just walking and seeing me because I am just there? Would he do the same and look at me if I was a man or a building or a dog? Trauma makes us struggle to be logical. It is okay, everyone has it. However, do improve your mindset and mental health. It is worth more than anything monetary item you can buy. Do not sit there and let it be.

If you can clock in eight hours a day, you can do the work to make yourself happier.

Examples of How I Reprogrammed My Brain to Love Myself

I had a deadline to finish five hundred words today but instead, I laid in bed and watched Netflix. Am I lazy or just tired because I worked eight hours today? I used to battle with myself and think I was useless and lazy because my mom primed me to degrade myself if I did not do enough. I do not even think I am lazy anymore. I started by writing out alternative positive thoughts for every negative thought I had. My internal monologue used to be "I am just a lazy person because I did nothing" to "I am lazy-... what a minute no I worked all week, woke up at seven am, cooked, and did laundry. It is ok if I am tired and want to rest because I am human and not a machine" to finally "hmm my body is telling me I need rest, I will make up for it on my day off on Saturday when I am well rested and write at the cafe patio while enjoying my favorite drink." I knew I was hard myself, but I did nothing to fix it. I realize a lot of people do this because it's how they are programmed, and they do not know how to fix it. I also realized growing up in an environment where they are constantly degraded programmed their brain to do this by themselves and it is almost comforting or soothing. Believing that the negative talk will make you better and work harder is only setting yourself up for failure.

If you are willing to change your thinking, you can change your life.

Here is a worksheet that I did every day for eight months in therapy. Let me use it as an example of when I have a negative or anxious thought about men because my father molested me.

Q.   Situation: Describe the event or thought that led to the unpleasant emotion
A.   My father molested me when I was ten years old.

Q.   Thought/ Stuck point: thought that I have from the event and rate belief from 0 to 100%
A.   All men are trash 80%.

Q.   Emotions felt and rate each emotion from 0 to 100%
A.   Anger 90%, Sadness 60%.

Q.   Use Challenging Questions to examine the thought
A.   Evidence for: my dad mistreated me, and I know some other men who disrespect women.

Evidence against: some men treat me well and are respectful to women like Frank.

Q.   Not including all information?
A.   Yes

Q.   All or none?
A   Yes

Q.   Extreme or exaggerated?
A   Yes

Q.   Focused on just one piece?
A   Yes, my dad

Q.   Source dependable?
A   Dependable

Q.   Confusing possible with likely?

A   Yes

Q.   Based on feelings or facts?

A   Both

Q   Focused on unrelated parts?

A   Yes

Q.   Problematic Patterns

A   Jumping to conclusions, exaggerating or minimizing, ignoring the
important part, oversimplifying, overgeneralizing, mind reading, emotional reasoning.

Q.   Alternative thought: what else can I say instead of the thought in section
A   A   How else can I interpret the event instead of this thought?
Rate the thought
      from 0 to 100%

A   Some men are trash; men can be trash because anyone can 40%.
Q.   Re-rate old thought/stuck point from 0 to 100% 60%

Q.   Emotion(s) felt and rate from 0 to 100%
A.   Defeated 20%, confused 10%, hopeful 5%

I completed this worksheet every day for eight months while seeking weekly
therapy, specifically diabolical behavioral therapy (DBT). DBT was the right fit
for me because of my diagnosis.

The worksheet helped me reprogram my thoughts surrounding my abuse. It
was understandable that I would think men are trash, but I did not actually want
that. I wanted to find a partner and being a straight female, I had to find a way
to not hate men. I was so traumatized from the event that I generalized every
man to be dangerous. I had to reprogram my brain to retrain it to be more logical for my own sake. The worksheet did that for me and practicing every day

allowed me to genuinely feel like some men are good and some men are bad, just like women. The traumatizing events usually lead to negative thoughts that are not facts which lead to bad habits. Instead of coping with substances, reaffirming my negative beliefs, and bottling my emotions up, I handled my trauma finally the right way and became stable. Therapy to understand my root problem taught me my father was not stupid and evil, he did something that was wrong. That made me change my thinking about men, for my own sake because I wanted to live in peace and find love. I improved my trauma surrounding my abuse from my father and hatred for all men substantially, due to therapy and completing worksheets every day to reprogram my brain.

You have to be willing to be logical and seek it constantly. Believe me, it is hard, but you can reprogram your brain to be what it was despite your trauma and become who you are meant to become. So put in the work and be stronger than your abuser.

I was diagnosed numerous times to get a diagnosis that felt right. Unfortunately, mental health is so hard to diagnose because there are so many diagnoses with similar symptoms. I was diagnosed with depression which did not feel right because I had mood changes. That led to my diagnosis of bipolar disorder which did not fit because I was never manic, I was happy for a few hours, but it did not last more than a few days. I got diagnosed with ADHD which did not even make sense, I did not struggle to focus more than the average person. I read about borderline personality disorder and for the first time, it felt right, and a psychiatrist confirmed my diagnosis. Some say the specific diagnosis does not matter but I disagree. I wanted to be medicated because I struggled to even want to live every day. I wanted to be on the right therapy because there are different types for different concerns. I was taking mood stabilizers when they thought I had bipolar disorder, but I still felt empty and sad every day. Then, I am taking serotonin boasters (SSRIs) which actually makes me feel better. However, I do not recommend anyone to rely on medication, it has to be combined with therapy and effort to become more stable every day. The medication made me survive while life was a mess, so I could focus on getting better. BDP is treated with DBT and SSRI, so I did that. Now, I am off medication, which was only possible because I relied on a combination of therapeutic sources, not just medication.

I fixed my everyday routine to live a healthy balanced lifestyle. The seemingly mundane suggestions that doctors suggest and nag about are there for a reason. Drinking enough water, eating three meals a day at the right time, waking up in the morning, sleeping at a reasonable time for eight hours, exercising, showering every day, and maintaining a clean space all exist for a reason, to make sure we live a balanced healthy life. Each of these individually can impact mental health.

Giving up is not an option, so you might as well thrive. Survivors make sure they can thrive.

At eighteen years old I was suicidal and prayed to God to let me go. I attempted to take my life three times. Then, my brain decides to piece it together and remember that I was sexually assaulted. I was homeless, jobless, hopeless, addicted to marijuana, and often spent my time in the forest crying uncontrollably every day. I was at my lowest point many times and I finally decided to choose myself. I chased my dream and sought my purpose, which was to live in the city and work in mental health. I took a leap of faith and only had enough money in my bank account for the first and last months of rent. I moved and found any job that hired me. I waitressed, worked in retail, and tutored to make ends meet. I went from having no energy to even live to being on fire because my environment changed. I got my dream job in mental health after months of trying and getting no interviews. I launched my own company and made the top two percent of sales of companies that launched the same month on Shopify. I was promoted to a full-time position as a primary caseworker in six months. I worked intensely on my mental health and changed my whole lifestyle to promote stable mental health. I am applying to Columbia University and New York University for my master's education. I found love with a man who showed me a stable, healthy relationship. This was all possible in one year because I chose myself, against my abusers, despite trauma, and I fought for my life. I am thankful for every tear that I felt because it led me to my passion, purpose, and a story to tell you to hopefully inspire you and help you.

Life starts when you choose yourself. Go get your life!

DEDICATION

I would like to dedicate this to all my friends and family who helped me on this journey of healing. I also dedicate this to all the readers who resonate with my words. Find life despite your hardships

Always pray to have
eyes that see the
best in people,
A heart that forgives
the worst,
A mind that forgets
the bad,
And a soul that never
loses faith in God.

A Blessing In Disguise

By: Amina Bhanji

Introduction

" Suffering is a gift, in it is hidden mercy" (by Rumi)

It was a beautiful, bright December morning with the birds chirping and the gentle glow of sunrise streaming through the open window. The sun warmed my room and brought in the fragrant scent of flowers. This day began just like any other day. Unknowingly, life was suddenly going to be catapulted into a new reality that day….

My early beautiful and simple childhood…

My name is Amina Bhanji, born Amina Valani. Amina in Arabic means 'loyal, trustworthy and honest'. It's funny, they say that the meaning of your name determines your personality and your destiny. Well, I have been told that my name is a perfect description of my personality, but I think I was "loyal to a fault." My mum nicknamed me "Mina" as a term of endearment, and so I am known as Mina in my immediate circle.

I was born in a small town called Shinyanga in Northern Tanzania and grew up in Dar-es-Salaam which means 'Abode of Peace' and indeed that is an accurate description of my homeland. Dar-es-Salaam is a beautiful, major city and commercial port located in Tanzania's Indian Ocean coast. This beautiful place dates back to 1857 and was the location of plantations where maize, millet and cassava was grown. I have many fond memories of my homeland, Africa, where it was warm all year round, close to the equator with 35-degree temperatures.

Vivid memories of my childhood go as far back as when I was six years old, reveling in the simple things in life. My humble family home reflected simplicity that welcomed family and joyful conversations. It was a two-story semidetached town house in the village of Kariakoo. We lived upstairs in a one-bedroom home, with a small kitchen, bathroom and common living and dining area. On the other side of the semi was my Aunt Zarina, her husband my uncle Aziz, my cousin and best friend Nuri and her younger sister Rishma. I loved to come home from school and play with Nuri as we were the same age with similar interests. I played with a compilation of dolls handmade by my talented Aunt Zarina, lovingly made for me and Nuri, out of basic household supplies. She used a popsicle stick for the body of the doll, a cotton ball for the head, and loose remnants of discarded fabric for the doll's clothing. Such simple things brought such simple pleasures in life back then.

I was the younger sister of five much older brothers, four of whom were married. They all lived in Dar-es-Salaam except for one of my elder brothers Shiraz. We were a very close knit, united and religious family who met regularly to share good times and good company. I looked forward to weekend sleepovers at my eldest brother Aziz's house. Aziz and his wife Mehrun were loving and kind to me since my childhood and treated me like a precious princess. On my birthdays, they had a big birthday party at their house, and they always arranged for a special pretty dress handmade just for me.

I enjoyed drinking sugar cane juice with ice in a big glass mug on boiling hot days walking along the beach. I remember my father walking with me on that long and winding road to school. My "Bapa'" treated me with this yummy, delicious drink on days that I missed the school bus. I wish those walks would never end. I can still taste that yummy mouth-watering juice in my mouth today.

Another one of my fondest memories was the simple home cooked food made by my mother - "Ma." Meals were composed of basic, local grocery ingredients, mainly lentils. Our family would have this delicious, nutritious meal every day with warm milk for dinner. It was called 'khichri'. Khichri is made of spiced dal with rice and is a vegan dish. It is a simple recipe made with moong dal (split mung beans), basmati rice, Indian spices with ghee or butter. Once you consume this, it will keep you full. This dish can be found on the Indian subcontinent and is meant to be easy to digest - a great comfort food for people living a humble life, as eating seafood, chicken or beef was considered a luxury. To this day it is one of my favourite dishes!

Big changes come overnight!

What came next was sudden, unbelievable, and confusing. Overnight, everything changed in my life from that carefree sunny December day. I had to leave my family and home behind and move into the unknown - a different country on a different continent.

I travelled to London, England with my brother Gulam, his wife Gulzar and their young son Alfin. My sister-in-law Mehrun and my brother Aziz travelled there earlier in August to get settled down. My parents Ma and Bapa stayed behind under the loving care of my middle brother Madat and sister-in-law Nasim. Unfortunately, my parents - Ma and Bapa, did not have the status to go outside of Africa and were too old to travel so suddenly. In the midst of all this commotion and confusion, this little girl, myself, was unaware I would be leaving Ma and Bapa, my friends and my whole WORLD behind! It was just that one day I was living this simple carefree life of mine, and the next, I was no longer living *in it. Just like that. No warning. Nothing.*

What was the reason behind this uprooting?

My forefathers and community were of South Asian descent. They were first uprooted from their original homeland, Gujarat, the fifth largest state in India. During the British colonial rule in Africa, manpower was needed to build the railroad system there. Our community lived in Africa for three generations, however in 1972, the then 'dictator' of Uganda expelled 80,000 of the country's Asians, apparently after receiving a 'message from God, in his dream' ordering the people to leave the country within 90 days!

This "ethnic cleansing'" soon spread to neighbouring Kenya and Tanzania where my family lived. Everyone's property and wealth were suddenly confiscated, their citizenship status downgraded, businesses were nationalized, people were harassed, livelihoods turned upside down, and their sense of belonging shattered and "gone just like the wind'.

It all happened as a flash of light.

My journey ahead starts….

My long journey to this new chapter began on an airplane. This was a new form of transportation for me. At this point, I had never even been in a car! The only transportation I knew was the local public bus that I took to travel on with Ma and Bapa. On this very first airplane ride I got very sick on the way. Finally, after what seemed like ages, the plane smoothly landed on this new unknown land. I had no idea that this was going to be my "new" home now.

I found myself now living in Mitcham Surrey, a small village in England, an hour's distance south of London. I stayed in a nice, cozy home with my brothers Aziz and Gulam, my sister in laws Mehrun and Gulzar, my nephew Alfin and my aunty Naseem, Mehrun's sister. This was my new home now with my extended family. A short while after my arrival there, my aunt Naseem suggested that since my brother Aziz and my sister-in-law Mehrun were taking care of me, why don't I call them "mum" and "dad", (as they were going to become my legal guardians for immigration purposes)? So, from then on, I called them mum and dad, and I still do to this day!

My new 'mum' Mehrun was a blessing, an angel sent to me by God. She was to dedicate her life to the well-being of others, as she was from a poor family, and although she was a very bright student, she had to leave high school after Grade 10 and work to support her family. At first looking after younger siblings in a family of ten, then raising her two much younger sisters Naseem and Naaz, after her parents passed away at a young age from cancer. She later got married and dedicated her life to her loving husband and his family, then raising two daughters who were children of family members taken under her care. Mum is one in a million! She's my motivator, comforter, inspiration, confidante, and best friend. She taught me the importance of compassion to others. She's been the light of my life and has shown me the right path to follow our ethics and valued traditions.

Mehrun's niece Shyrose, joined us in London a year later from Africa and was legally adopted by Aziz and Mehrun. She was now my elder sister. I was happy to have a sister as I didn't have any sisters, or any siblings close to my own age. We became close and still are today. She always took good care of me through all the different stages in my life. Alfin, even though his parents lived with us, also called Aziz and Mehrun mum and dad and was now considered my younger brother. At first, I attended private school in England with Shyrose and Alfin. I can still remember we paid one penny at recess for a chocolate finger as a snack – yum! I can still taste it till today!

Later in 1974, I moved to a different part of the country - Croydon, to live with my brother Gulam's family, with the addition of my new nephew Alnoor. They now became the parental figures in my life. Gulam owned a grocery store where we lived in the upper floor, so all my tasty snacks for school were on the house from then on. There I learned many things, including how to say our daily prayers in Arabic from my sister-in-law Gulzar.

Another big change comes along!

Life flowed naturally and beautifully as I got used to living in my new world. But alas, just when I got used to living in England, in September of 1975, another big change in my life occurred. I didn't realize that living in England was just a temporary residence as we did not have permanent residency there. I had to take yet another long plane ride over the ocean to another different continent with my sister Shyrose. This time my destination was to Toronto, Ontario, the most populous city in Canada.

I was nine years old at the time. My parents Aziz and Mehrun had immigrated there from England in July of 1975 to settle down in the "new land of opportunity" and prepared to call the rest of the family there. I was excited to reunite with them again and be in their welcoming arms for a tight hug that I missed! I especially missed my mum playing with my hair and giving me a head massage with warm oil, then tying my hair in two braids. These were loving moments that still warm my heart.

Canada, the new land, was a desirable English-speaking country to emigrate to. Everyone was welcome to go there to start a new life, as the then Prime Minister opened his arms wide to all including my South Asian community. All was based on humanitarian grounds, as Canada brought many great opportunities to all, such as free public education, learning the English language, a fantastic no charge health care system, a great pension plan, employment insurance and so many other benefits.

Unbelievable! But all was not as perfect as it seemed. Many of the immigrants' qualifications to work in Canada were either minimal or not recognized. A lot of immigrants lacked the required "Canadian experience'" which was a huge employment barrier. Most had arrived with little or no money and absolutely no possessions. They just HAD to find employment immediately for the basic necessities to feed their families and provide shelter.

These immigrants made many sacrifices where they went through hardships for this new life in a strange new country, where the weather was cold, and most had language barriers. This was NOTHING like the life they were used to in Africa, where the men were middle class businessmen. Now the women had to work, upgrade themselves and be required to perform chores they were not required to do in Africa. They were used to being regular housewives in Africa, where each home employed domestic help to come in daily to support in making meals, looking after children, cleaning and basic household chores.

Life goes on…

Our own family underwent these same challenges. Mehrun found a job in the municipal government as a secretary within a week of coming to Canada. She was fortunate to find it, as she was knowledgeable with the English language, had shorthand and secretarial skills she had obtained while living in England, where Aziz opened his own print shop called Printka. He later went on to become a very successful Real Estate Agent.

Out of the 1.5 billion fathers in the world, I can confidently say that my dad is not just the best dad, he's the best DAD EVER! As the eldest son, he too had to leave high school to support his poor family. He looked after his two younger brothers growing up. Although biologically he is my eldest brother, he took me in as his own child, due to the political crisis in Africa. He also has spent the last 50 years giving me, and my entire family the best life ever, keeping us strong and united. For a man who didn't finish high school to support his family, he has earned the highest sales awards time and again as a real estate agent. Not only is he an amazing salesman, but he is also outstanding in math. He has a heart of gold, is a man of integrity and one of the most generous and caring souls. He has helped countless people over the years, not just our family, and people from our community, but also many needy families that we don't even know. For example, he reached out and partnered with other family, friends and people from our community to help raise funds to sponsor 7 families to Toronto from Syria in 2017, to give them a new life. This included getting help to fill out their immigration papers, helping them get jobs, finding a place to stay, getting their children into the school system, and all other basic needs for their first year here in Toronto.

It takes a village to raise a child

Mehrun and Aziz sponsored both sides of their families to come to Canada successfully. Members of their families eventually immigrated to Canada and lived with us right until they obtained their own jobs and settled down with their own families.

I learned to make new friends and start a new life again. The Ismaili community was a very close one and there was always someone there to lend a helping hand. We grew up initially in the west end of the Greater Toronto area where many other Ismaili families lived. For the first time in my life I lived in an apartment building and felt a sense of community. I walked to and from school in large groups with my close Ismaili friends who lived there; while in Grade four, I ate lunch with them and played after school with them. I always felt safe and protected in this community. We attended Jamat Khana (Ismaili Muslim place of worship) daily, so I became habituated to practicing my faith regularly and trying to live an ethical life. To me, that means that everything you do needs to be aligned with our faith, our values and our beliefs. There is no dichotomy between faith and our daily life.

Then in 1976 we moved to another neighbourhood in the west end of Toronto where there were not as many Ismailis living there. It was a very different experience. I was discriminated against, at first in England's public school system and now in Canada. I was pushed around and called a "Paki" by my class bullies. I was teased for having an English accent that I picked up while in London and lost it swiftly to fit in. I felt like I was being silenced from speaking and expressing myself freely.

I remember vividly one incident when I was in grade five at ten years old. I had been assigned a small but important task of walking a little girl to school for extra pocket money. Her parents trusted me with their child and paid me $5 per week. The little Kindergarten girl was called Rita. I carefully held Rita's hand guiding her as I walked her to school daily. I will never forget that freezing winter morning when something awful happened. There had been a large snowfall the night before and everything was covered in white snow. All of a sudden, a group of four girls, including a girl in my class that bullied me, appeared out of nowhere. They physically pushed both Rita and I backwards onto the front yard of a resident's house on our route home from school. Then they came towards us standing over our bodies yelling racial slurs at us loudly. I tried to protect Rita but was unsuccessful. The deed was done. Rita started crying uncontrollably and I felt completely helpless and scared. I never told anyone. Not my parents. Not her parents. Not the teachers. No one. Out of fear of what may happen.

Finally together at last!

The rest of my immediate family later joined us in stages, as they required official immigration paperwork to come to Canada. My brother Madat and sister-in-law Nasim, with their two daughters Farzana and Shezadi came to Toronto in October of 1977 from Africa. They always loved me and helped me in any way I needed with their guidance, support and affection till today. Then my birth mum and dad - Ma and Bapa arrived from Africa in February of 1978. My brother Gulam and his family did not get their immigration papers to come to Canada from England in 1975 with us, so they went to live in Portugal, and then Alfin came to Canada in the fall of 1978 and the rest of his family followed in May of 1979. I was very happy to be finally reunited with the rest of my family after many years of separation. Eventually we all got our permanent residence for Canada and then became Canadian citizens.

I was raised with so much love that I was totally oblivious of all the hardships my family and community went through! My eyes were opened to the experiences of my family and community when I researched this historic incident for my Toastmaster's speech. I read Mansoor Ladha's book "*Memoirs of a Muhindi, fleeing East Africa for the West.*" I also learned a lot from Omar Sachedina, a reporter from my Ismaili community, who did a documentary in 2022 about his family's personal experience leaving Uganda, to mark the 50th anniversary of their plight. It was called *"Omar Sachedina: My Roots in Uganda."*

Serving my Ismaili community – something I am very proud of!

Serving and the spirit of volunteerism is one of the pillars of our faith. My mum was always involved with volunteering in our Jamat Khana (Ismaili Muslim place of worship) and eventually was appointed as a "Co- Major", now called "Director'" of a volunteer organization in my community in the early eighties.

Not surprisingly, I was blessed to follow her footsteps and was appointed as a "Co-Major" from 1992 - 1994. We oversaw approximately 2,400 volunteers across 24 centers in Ontario at the time. It's funny but I never intended to move up that ladder to the top. I just followed my heart and did what made me happy, and success followed. It's like the Universe knew that I was meant to be a leader and created these opportunities to nudge me along, but I just didn't know it yet.

Today, I am proud to say that I am a Canadian Ismaili Muslim, and we are grateful to Canada for the great opportunities given to us to thrive! Although back in 1972 it was considered a nightmare for me. Now as someone who has lived through such an ordeal, the "Dream from God" that the Dictator had in my opinion was '**A Blessing in Disguise**', hence the title of my chapter in this book.

Finally, a place to call home!

We FINALLY have an amazing place to call 'home'! As they say, "Home is where the heart is". My kids are getting a good education and have a good quality of life. We are blessed with everything we need, a far cry from my humble beginnings in Africa. There is a bright future ahead for us in our Ismaili Community! We are now respectable professionals and contributing members of society, giving back to the Canadian community through a strong work ethic and voluntary service. We have a voice in this country. NONE of this would be possible if Canada had not opened its doors to the Ismaili Community 51 years ago! THANK YOU, CANADA! We love you for your big heart, for welcoming diversity, upholding the values of compassion, equality, respect, dignity and peace. We can move forward into a peaceful, positive and hopeful future now!

Your pain is the catapult to your purpose!

"Where there is pain, the cure will come" (by Rumi)

I was always proud that I was like my mother, a kind, caring and giving person (at least that's what I have been told). Little did I realize that although those are good qualities to have, you cannot be too kind or too giving. You need to know your worth when dealing with people, as not everyone will value you, and there is a risk of being used. My mum upheld her self-worth to protect herself. Unfortunately, I did not do that by being around "energy vampires". I did not know the term "energy vampires" until one day my career coach Anne Rose used it as part of a conversation with me. I became curious and read a book called *"Dodging Energy Vampires"* by Dr. Christiane Northrup. I learned a lot and would like to share my findings with you here.

"When you dim your own heart to please others, the whole world gets darker."(by Dr. Christiane Northrup)

"Who are Energy Vampires?"

"Energy Vampires" can be "Narcissists" who are toxic people, that literally suck the life blood out of you. Being with them often leaves you drained, depleted and tired! They PREY on the trust of empaths as they are chameleons and master manipulators in getting what they want! They don't recognize the needs and feelings of others, feeling superior to them as though they are entitled. These are selfish people, lacking true compassion and remorse, exhibiting vengeful behaviour and anger. They are deceitful, being comfortable around trauma, drama and chaos that they create. They don't feel guilty as they think they are perfect, so nothing is wrong with them. They make themselves look like the victims and make empaths feel like they are at fault.

Empaths versus "Energy Vampires"

Empaths are approval seeking, people pleasing, codependent and self-sabotaging people who see life through compassion and caring; they are deeply concerned about the well-being of others and that is how they are 'designed' from birth. They open their hearts to help people heal their wounds by over-giving, without including their own needs and well-being! That is their primary weakness. I learned that I am an empath and that was one of my weaknesses.

There are positives to the empath, as they are natural healers who can help people feel safe, seen and heard. *"Dodging Energy Vampires"* showed tips, techniques, and tactics to LEAVE these harmful relationships behind, heal from them and let your own light shine. A big lesson for me here! I learned that you have to identify the "energy vampires" in your life, whether they are your friends, family, coworkers, neighbours. or even strangers who cut you off in traffic; then understand why you seem to attract vampires in your life, time and again!

I also learned about the dynamics of a vampire and empath relationship, which is clearly a **perfect storm**!

Empaths are the prey of "energy vampires" who feed off their energy to disrupt their lives. Empaths lose their health (physical, mental and emotional), their self-esteem and dignity in the process of this relationship. Since it is a codependent relationship without boundaries, the narcissists use manipulation to control and dominate the relationship. Whereas the empath takes on the submissive role. The co-dependent empath under values themselves, while the narcissist over values themselves. Empaths are loyal, patient people looking for acceptance and believe in the goodness of others. When a relationship is not a healthy one, problems no doubt arise. Empaths are forever giving, and narcissists are forever taking, causing imbalance in the "give and take'" of the relationship. Empaths continue to allow energy vampires to treat them badly, with disrespect, accept their lies, manipulation and deceit. They continue to believe that they're not good enough, and this codependency, back and forth roller coaster continues as a vicious cycle.

I am an Empath!

Are you an empath? Chances are, if you are still reading this you probably are one or know someone who is. Guess what? I am proud to call myself an empath! I now know not take on the burden of other people energetically, so it can be a superpower that makes you remarkable and vulnerable. I discovered that a few of my close relationships for a long time, both in my personal and professional life are with toxic people. After reading "*Dodging Energy Vampires,*" a veil was lifted, and I could finally see clearly for the first time in my life! I learned to see these toxic people for their true colours "behind their mask" and I distanced from them completely to protect myself. I used to try to justify myself and get caught up in their drama by reacting emotionally. They get a kick out of getting us to react, so <u>the best response is no response at all</u>. I had to learn to not be so defensive, to NOT REACT and NOT FEEL A NEED to justify myself! I had to stop believing that I was less than what I was made to feel! Like many other empaths, I missed the "red flags" by not being in tune with my intuition. Also, my desire to be accepted, to please others, and NOT HURT people, caused me to continue with these toxic relationships. Lastly, I stayed STUCK in this situation, as I genuinely believed I could help heal these people. I chose to continue to give my energy to them, at the risk of standing up for myself and owning how angry, hurt, resentful and disappointed I was! I realized I was codependent. I became insecure, anxious and fearful, stepping on eggshells in every move, because I was made to feel that way. I basically gave up my power and became a victim.

What I Learned....

I learned that toxic people don't change, only YOU can change! You need to know that enough is enough and you need to get out of the relationship ASAP! It is the only solution to get your peace of mind and life back! Once you recognize how "energy vampires" operate you are less likely to be victimized. I learned that it is not one's job to change people. They are who they are, and only they can change themselves if they want to. Therefore, if you cannot get along with this type of person, disassociate from them completely. If the relation is such that you have to continue with it, then draw strong boundaries and stick to them by being consistent. My kids taught me to have boundaries and to identify what it is that I want and don't want and to communicate it to others accordingly.

My Healing Journey....

Being an empath, I was naïve in trusting others thinking that they were honest like me, but I was wrong. My trust was broken and my confidence and self-worth shattered. I realize that this happened because I allowed it to happen, and although I forgive myself for it, I am much wiser now and more cautious. I am not as gullible anymore, and one will need to earn my trust going forward. I will never let anyone hurt or disrespect me again. Never. I give my energy only to those people who are positive and genuinely care for my highest good. I am still in the process of my healing journey, but at least I have my freedom and peace of mind back! I control my own life on my own terms, instead of being a puppet dangling to the tune of someone else's terms. I am grateful that I have a family and friends who love and accept me for exactly who I am, and I know who my rocks are! My rocks are the people that I can call even at 2 a.m. and they will be there for me no matter what!

Moving On!

The theme of this book *'Empowered in Heels'* Edition 3 is "*Living with a Purpose,*" it is all about using your experience to help others. This is what I wish to do moving forward by starting with writing this chapter in this book. I always knew my purpose was pegged to helping people, so I followed "Human Resources" as a career path. However, it did not fulfill me, as it helps people, but there are conflict resolution issues that I am not comfortable with.

Then I saw this post on Facebook. It said:

"Good Karma – Note to Self"
"*What is my purpose in life?*" I asked the void.

"What if I told you that you fulfilled it when
you took an extra hour to talk to that kid about
his life?" said the voice.
"Or when you paid for that young couple in
the restaurant? Or when you saved that dog in
traffic? Or when you tied your father's shoes
for him?"

"Your problem is that you equate your purpose
With goal-based achievement. The Universe
isn't interested in your achievements. Just
your heart. When you chose to act out of
kindness, compassion and love, you
are already aligned with your true purpose."

This message really struck me emotionally.

One line in it reminded me that I used to tie my Bapa's shoelaces for him for the last five years of his life, as he couldn't because he was old, and he had cancer. I did it because I loved him, and it made me happy to help him. It made me realize that my purpose is not necessarily pegged to my career path, or ONLY ONE monumental thing that I needed to do in life. It could be _many_ different "little" meaningful things over my lifetime that I did from my heart. I believed everyone has a unique gift and our purpose was pegged to it.

Follow your bliss!

"Heart Alight: When you find your purpose, it is like your heart has been set alight with passion. You know it absolutely without any doubt." (By Rhonda Byrne)

Then I read the book *"The Secret"* by Rhonda Byrne and in it she quoted Joseph Campbell as saying, *"Follow your bliss."* To follow your bliss, is to do what you love, what you are passionate about, and follow your purpose.

After working closely with my dear friend and Career Coach Anne Rose in 2016, I decided to become certified as a Trainer and a Life Coach as I knew I wanted to help people. She made me go through a series of tests to find the right career path for me and go through a self-discovery exercise in her book *"Ignite: Your Purpose, Your Passion, Your Strengths, Your Vision."* We started with identifying my values, needs, strengths, and passions? What I loved to do and what makes me happy? What value they provide and what difference they make in my life? Then we aligned my passions with my purpose. How could I use my talents, skills, hobbies and interests to create positive change and inspire others? Let me share my passions with you on my journey to finding my purpose......

My first passion is fund raising for worthy causes close to my heart. In 2002, when I was an Assistant Manager at a major bank in Canada, a few members of my community who worked at the bank, walked to raise funds in Toronto in 2001. I was led by my intuition to create and lead multiple teams at various branches in cities across Canada, in support of the **Aga Khan Foundation's World Partnership Walk (WPW).** The walk held in multiple cities in Canada is the world's largest public movement to fight global poverty. I continued my volunteer efforts leading this nation-wide initiative from 2001 to 2006, then I passed it on to another Ismaili bank employee to lead it going forward. When I spoke with my WPW contact recently, I was overjoyed to learn that this bank and its employees have supported World Partnership Walk (WPW), since 2001 through sponsorships, team fundraising, and employee matching programs, totaling over **$3 million** to date! It is impressive to note that the bank's teams have raised over half of that total with **$1,742,191.00** in support of global development. Can you believe it? From sending a generic email over my lunch hour back in 2002 to other bank employees, that I didn't even know across the country, resulted in this outstanding miracle over time by 2023? The universe did everything to align people, circumstances and events to create this profound legacy. I am forever grateful & humbled for this opportunity!

My second passion is public speaking. Feeling like I was silenced in the past, I now feel like I can speak freely and openly through this powerful medium. I learned that two of my gifts are my leadership and my communication skills, so I became a Toastmasters in 2011. Now 13 years later, from countless amazing leadership opportunities, I earned the eighth and highest award designation from **Toastmasters International,** to be a "*Distinguished Toastmasters*" (DTM) after 9 years of hard work, but I also made some of my closest friends. One of the most fulfilling experiences for me, was to be the coordinator for the "*Youth Leadership Program*" in 2017. With the help of my friends, family and Toastmasters family, I facilitated this Toastmasters communication and leadership program over two sessions to 40 Ismaili youth in the Greater Toronto Area. The other great honour for me was to give a toast to Canada at the "*George Keenan Awards Luncheon*" at the <u>2019 District 60 Toastmaster's Conference</u>, where I shared my story briefly about leaving Africa during a political crisis and thanking Canada for welcoming my family and community to this great land of opportunity.

My third passion is teaching. Did I mention that I majored in English to become an English Teacher, but I didn't get into the Teaching Program? Well, that is what lead me to further my education in Human Resources. Now I am a certified Trainer to teach adults.

In 2019, I started volunteering as a Tutor in Math and English with a few friends and family for the **Refugee Women's Network (RWN),** which made us very happy and feel like we were making a difference to these women's lives. It is an organization that empowers refugee and immigrant women by helping them rebuild their lives through education. They help women through their settlement by providing sustainable skills to enable them to support their families, to advocate for their children and to support aging family members.

From 2020 to 2021 during Covid-19, I was an online volunteer English teacher to a young 13-year-old boy in India. This amazing experience brought me so much happiness and a world of fulfillment, not only in teaching him and learning from him, but also in making friendships with dedicated volunteer teachers globally. This was a collaborative project called "*Hakuna Mipaka*" which in Swahili means "*No Limits, No Boundaries*" between the **Acts of Love Foundation** and **FlowGlowGrow**.

Acts of Love (AOL) is a non-profit organization that strives to provide a better life to marginalized children and families in Gujerat, India. As you know, my own family and many members of our Ismaili community were originally from Gujerat, so I have always wanted to pay it forward. Munira Nagji the founder of AOL truly is an inspiration and the second Mother Teresa for India, and I am in total awe of her sacrifices, compassion and kindness. Neelam Hirji, an Elementary School Teacher and the Founder of FlowGlowGrow offers various tailored services to improve mental and emotional health as well as the overall well-being of children, adults, educators and corporate workers.

My fourth passion is coaching people. What is coaching and what does a Life Coach do you ask? Well quite simply, a life coach is someone who counsels and encourages clients through personal and or professional challenges. They help guide their clients to reach their goals through behaviour changes, shifting perspectives and overall self-improvement. From 2019-2022, I was a volunteer Employment Coach with my Ismaili community, helping people with building their resumes, interview preparation and looking for suitable employment. Now, I am a Certified Life Coach.

Once I knew my passions, skills and talents and I followed them, my purpose revealed itself to me in the process of my journey over time. I am particularly drawn to vulnerable children, women and seniors. I initially realized my purpose was called to kindness somehow. When I started a kindness initiative at my work in 2016, with my coworkers, we made candy grams with a smiley face button to thank staff in support of our local United Way of Greater Toronto, a not-for-profit organization fighting local poverty. From 2017- 2020, I joined the Employee Engagement Committees at my work with the Ontario Public Service to promote kindness at work through different initiatives.

In 2018, I became a "RAKtivist." A Kindness Activist for the Random Acts of Kindness Foundation (RAOK) and still am till today. Their mission is to inspire people to practice kindness as a "norm" and to "pass it on" to others. As a Kindness Activist, each year I promote kindness by posting messages all month long on Facebook in honour of **Random Act of Kindness Day** on *February 17th* and for the **World Kindness Day** on *November 13th.* I am honoured that I was selected as one of thirty people worldwide by the RAOK to go to the United States as part of their Kindness Conference, but due to the COVID-19 outbreak, it was unfortunately cancelled.

I am sharing these examples of following my passion with you, so you can see how I found my purpose, and how you can hopefully find your purpose too, so you CAN feel like you can make a difference as well. The universe is designed to multiply every good action we do, to create ripple effects on countless people from 1 single random act of kindness. It takes minutes a day, to consciously decide what we will do to make a difference. It's not the size or monetary value of your act of kindness, it is the lasting impression on people you reach. You can make a difference. We are all born to make the world a better place. I hope I have inspired you to ask, *"what will you do today to make this world a better place?"*

The last few years during the pandemic brought extra challenges my way: I fell and tore the meniscus in both my knees, which has restricted me from many of my daily activities; then my dad's health declined, and I had to help my mum look after him, and move closer to them; in the interim, I have gone through the painful process of a separation; and lastly, I have been looking after my uncle, (my Ma's brother) for two years, since he went into a nursing home. I am from the "*sandwich generation*" like many others are today, where we are middle aged people, caring for both our elderly parents and our own children. This can be rewarding no doubt, but also quite challenging.

All of these factors happening simultaneously took a toll on me, and I had to cut back on my passions like volunteering, hobbies and Toastmasters to cope with them. I was not able to manage juggling everything on top of my normal day to day responsibilities of working fulltime, going to school part-time at this age, and being a mother of two daughters. I was overwhelmed, stressed and burnt out. I had to prioritize my life around the things that mattered the most. Those being my family, my health and my faith (my physical, mental, emotional and spiritual well-being).

This led me to realize that at this point in time in my life, THIS was my purpose. I also realized that by doing everything for everyone else and NOT looking after MYSELF, I was doing a disservice to ME. As an empath you feel other people's energy which drains you, so I had to learn to protect my energy and be restrictive with my time, energetically, emotionally and physically. I could not afford to agree to do things I was not able to. At first, it was really hard for me to say "*no*" but slowly I got more comfortable and felt less guilty.

As an empath, I absorbed other people's energies, so at the end of the day I felt exhausted, irritated and disconnected from myself. By learning to carve out time for myself, to relax, to have some "*me time,*" to read or do whatever soothed me, made me feel like I was showing up for myself, and not just everyone else. When I learned to schedule in a little "*self-care*" for myself, that lead me to realize my "NEW" purpose. Recently, I learned that you can only show kindness to others when you show it to YOURSELF FIRST! Therefore, I created my new "*Kindness through Self Care*" website. It includes the important topics of self-care, self-respect, self-worth, self-empowerment and so much more!

Lessons Learned, messages worth sharing…

1. **Know your worth**! Have self-confidence. Pat yourself on the back regularly. Don't believe what others tell you by putting you down. Our self-confidence only shatters when we give too much attention to the opinions of others, rather than trusting our own inner guidance and intuition.

2. **Stand up for yourself**. Speak your truth and honour your feelings. Have courage. Trust yourself. You're stronger than you realize. Take that leap of faith and don't let your anxieties and fears hold you back. Get rid of those limiting beliefs and self-doubt, replacing them with positive affirmations.

3. **Know your boundaries**. Learn the power of NO, to identify and ask for what it is that you want and communicate it to others.

4. **Fill your own cup FIRST**. You can't pour from an "empty cup." Focus on you - put yourself first without guilt. Don't over-give and forget yourself in the process. Rest. Rejuvenate. Relax. Recalibrate. Avoid burnout and anxiety.

5. **Don't allow negativity in your energy field**. People who put you down and have a harsh critical energy towards you, let them go. Clear old energy regularly. Do not accept disrespect from anyone.

6. **Release your emotions in a healthy way**. Don't bottle them up. Allow yourself to feel whatever emotions arise within you to give them a voice. Even cry if it helps you release what no longer serves you. Once they are released, you will feel lighter.

7. **Accept that people don't change unless they want to**. If they did it once they'll do it again. Look at their behaviour not their words. It is not our responsibility to change anyone except ourselves.

8. **You are ENOUGH**! Not everyone has to like you and that is ok. You don't have to be a people pleaser to get them to like or accept you. Stand as the light you are.

9. **Be YOU unapologetically and love yourself**! Go forward with grace and compassion. YOU are number #1! Remember you are beautiful. This experience is just a phase to help you grow.

What did I do to heal? (What has been therapeutic for me?)

1.   Step away from stress, tension, over thinking, worrying, fearing, doubt, limiting beliefs and self-sabotage. One way is to breathe deeply and regularly, as our breath is directly related to our stress levels.

2.	Be loving and kind to myself and others. Gift myself with peace through alone quiet time, to slow down, to go at my own pace, rest, reflect, reserve my energy, and give back to myself; to spend time in nature, especially by walking near water and trees.

3.	Trust in God and know that the universe has my back. To surrender control through meditation, prayer, and reconnecting with my inner guidance and spirit.

4.	Journal to express my thoughts, in fact, writing this chapter in this book has been very cathartic and therapeutic for my own healing journey.

5.	Follow my intuition, express my creativity and help others. It is my intent to achieve this through creating my kindness through self-care website.

6.	Setting boundaries with people around me. If they are not in alignment with me then I distance myself. I don't allow people to put me down and question my worth anymore.

7.	Following the suggestions in the "Dodging Energy Vampires" book.

8.	Reaching out to my family and friends, spending time with them, feel their love, be willing to receive offers to help me when needed.

9.	Seeking help from those who are more experienced or professionals in their field.

10.	Adding a gratitude practice to my daily routine. I learned to thank the people who hurt me for teaching me lessons. Although the process was very painful for me, I gained clarity, freedom and peace from it and it made me stronger and wiser.

11.	Doing something for myself, mind, body and soul every day, even if only for 10 mins.

12.	Forgiving others and myself. I pray for those who hurt me and don't hold any grudges anymore. What you put out into the world comes back to you positive and negative. Find that little boy or girl inside of you that allowed this pain to happen and forgive them.

When Suzy Tamasy the creator of this book *"Empowered in Heels"* invited me to include my story in her next edition of this book, my ego felt scared. I wanted to say, *"no"*, *what do I have to say that the world will want to hear?"* My higher self and leaned into my intuition leading me to say "*YES!*" I felt called to use my voice and share my story, my experiences and most importantly, the lessons I learned from being in toxic relationships, and how I found my purpose through following my passions. Even if this helps *one* person, I will feel that it made a difference. We are all struggling in our own lives, in our own ways, and we all need to be kinder to ourselves and to each other, to help each other through these challenges to thrive again.

If you are feeling pain, let it flow through you, so it's not trapped inside. No matter how much people throw stones at you, get back up. You may feel like you're in a dark cave. The darkness holds the light that you seek. Find your purpose through your pain. Allow yourself to be still and meditate. It will bring you the clarity you need to move forward with love rather than fear. You are special and unique. Don't be afraid and don't let anyone make you suffer in silence anymore. Use your voice to teach and express the truth about your pain and share the lessons you've learned to others. Your suffering was not in vain. You are being called to raise awareness from your suffering. You got this!

In the final analysis, all my experiences were blessings in disguise. I thank God, my family and friends who helped me through my challenges and gave me hope for the future. Are you someone who gives too much to others and doesn't think about their own needs? Are you an empath? Are you codependent? Are you or have you been in a toxic relationship? If yes, I want to support you every step of the way so please feel free to go to my *"Kindness through Self Care"* website in the link below as I share many great ways to take better care of yourself. I look forward to hearing from you soon!

https://kindnessthroughselfcare.ca

DEDICATION

I would like to dedicate this chapter to my parents Aziz & Mehrun Valani, I love you and thank you for giving me a beautiful life, ethical values and treasured memories. You have been the best role models to me, and that is why I have a strong desire to help people. They say your soul chooses your parents before you're born. I must have been very wise to have picked not only ONE set of loving parents, but TWO sets of the best parents anyone could have ever asked for.

I'd also like to dedicate this chapter to my daughters Iman Bhanji & Rayna Bhanji, thank you for giving me strength and teaching me so much, including drawing boundaries and how to identify my needs and communicating them to others. I love you and I'm so very proud of you. Continue to be strong, unique, humble, kind and shine your light brightly in this world, leaving a legacy behind to make the world a better place.

I would also like to thank the following family and friends for helping me put the facts together in writing this chapter and providing their feedback: my aunt Nasim Kanji, my sister-in-law Nasim Valani, my nieces Farzana Bhanji & Shezadi Khushal, my brother Gulam Valani, my nephew Alfin Valani, my aunt Azmina Kassam, my close friends Ahalya Srikanthan, Renata Love, Shehnaz Abdulla, Nermin Sunderji, Nasreen Sevany, Errol Knight, Patrice Esper and Sutha Shanmugarajah.

Many thanks to those who were a great resource for my background research namely: Mansoor Ladha, Omar Sachedina, Kate Swift & Azin Soltani. Special thanks to Brooke Jones, Zein Dhanidina, Munira Nagji & Neelam Hirji for allowing me to use my experiences with their organizations as examples in the book.

Thank you, Suzy Tamasy, for the opportunity to write this chapter to share my story and providing guidance and support throughout the process.

Lastly, a final thanks to Anne Rose my Career Coach and dear friend for always being there for me, her vote of confidence, helping me find my calling in my career path and helping me write this book from the very first words.

Amina as a baby in Africa.

Amina at her brother Aziz's house in Africa.

Amina tutoring a women in English.

Amina promoting kindness at work during 'Pink Shirt Day'.

Amina giving a 'Toast to Canada' at the district 60 Toastmasters Conference in 2019

Amina's 2 amazing daughters Iman & Rayna

DON'T FEAR
FAILURE. FEAR
BEING IN THE
EXACT SAME
PLACE NEXT YEAR
AS YOU ARE
TODAY.

Her Courage Was Her Crown, And She Wore It Like a Queen

By Jennifer Middleton

I was born and raised in a small town in Saskatchewan. I grew up on the family farm that has been in our family for over 100 years. I am a mom of 4 amazing children. They mean the world to me. They have been my light when I saw darkness. They are my strength when I am weak. They have given me so much and have made me feel unconditional love. I am a certified Reiki Master, Karuna Reiki Master, Author, Certified Hypnotherapist, NLP Results Coach, Certified in Timeline Therapy and a Restaurant Manager.

When I was 2 years old, I went out to collect the eggs from my parents' chicken coop, we had chickens and geese. I don't really remember; my mom and dad had told me I was attacked by the gander. To this day we are unsure of how I survived this attack. My dad heard me crying and came running. The gander was on my back pecking me really hard. When dad and I got to the house, mom looked me over. I had some pretty bad bruises even though I had 3 layers of clothing on, as it was a cooler fall day. I definitely had a guardian angel watching over me that day. I still am not sure how the gander just managed to bruise my back and not get my face or the front of me. At the age of 2 I had my very first traumatic experience. Trust me this was the start of a whole lot of traumas and a lot of unhealed wounds.

As I grew up and became school age, I went to school. I started when I was 4 and turned 5 a little while after that. My school years were not the most memorable. I was bullied by my peers and told I would never amount to anything by my grade one teacher. I remember one certain thing; it was my birthday and my parents had gotten me a peach track suit for my birthday. I opened my birthday gift that morning and decided to wear my new outfit to school to show friends what my parents had gotten me for my birthday. I was very excited about my new outfit. I had gym class towards the end of the school day. I quickly changed into my gym clothes as we only had a short amount of time to change and be in the gym before we were late and had to get a late slip. I believe we were playing floor hockey or volleyball that day. As gym class came to an end, we were on our way to change out of our gym clothes and get ready to go home from school, when I got to where I had hung my clothes, I noticed they were not there. I was panicking and crying as I needed to change to catch the bus to get home. I couldn't find my clothes anywhere. I went to my teacher crying as they were my new clothes that I had just gotten for my birthday that morning. My teacher came in and she found them in the toilet. Some girls in my class had flushed my new clothes down the toilet. I was so upset. I had to get my teacher to take my clothes and put them in a plastic bag and I had to wear my gym clothes home. It was a cooler fall day. As I got home all ready to celebrate my birthday with my parents and grandparents, I had to explain to them why I was in my gym clothes. My birthday that year was not a very memorable one with happy memories. I learned after this not to wear my new birthday clothes to school again. I never did.

As school continued the bullying got worse and worse. I had a couple real good friends in school, and we hung out a lot. During school, I was a very dedicated figure skater in the winter. I enjoyed figure skating and learning all the new jumps and twirls and fancy things that figure skaters do. I was a fast learner. I enjoy figure skating, until the jealousy of a couple other figure skaters started to cause me to feel that I wasn't good at it. I was not into the competitions as other skaters were. I was quite content to just skate for fun and perform in our yearly carnival at the end of the skating year. Again, the bullying started. I was teased that I was too scared to do competitions and that I wasn't good enough any way to do competitions. I wasn't scared to do them. I was just happy skating for fun. After a few years of being teased and bullied in figure skating, I quit as I just didn't feel the same about it. My passion for skating was gone. I tried curling after this, and it was not for me. My parents and brother were avid curlers, and they were pretty good. My brother's team did really well. It just was not my calling.

Most of my childhood was spent on the farm helping my parents and grandparents out. My favourite time of the year was calving season. This did not come without challenges either. It was a very intense, highly emotional time of year. I recall a couple times myself feeling what my parents were feeling. I could not figure out why I remember my parents getting up every 3 hours to check on the cows and bring the calves in when it was cold. My grandfather drove out to help my dad as my brother and I were not quite old enough at the time and my mom was a nurse working nurses' hours. My parents were so tired during this time. My brother and I spent a lot of time with my grandparents. We became remarkably close with our grandparents. Some of my family would say we were their favourites. I never felt that way at all. I would feel the jealousy and the smart remarks from some family members. It did take its toll on me. I started to think very low of myself and I didn't want to be around or see my extended family. I would just stay home and work on my schoolwork or read books and avoid them as much as I could. My self esteem was very low. I was bullied in school and some family members were jealous of my relationship with my grandparents.

After I quit figure skating and decided curling was not for me, I saw an advertisement about karate. They had a demonstration going on and I was really interested in it. I went and participated and really enjoyed it. As fall came around, our recreation board offered karate. I was very excited about this; I asked my parents if I could take karate and they agreed. Karate changed my life and introduced me to a whole new chapter in my life. I took karate for just over 10 years. I spent my junior high and high school years in a karate dojo and competing in tournaments. My sensei and his family became my second family. I always referred to my sensei and his wife as my second dad and mom. As I started to advance and get really good at karate and competing in tournaments and winning medals the bullying tapered off.

Karate was my introduction to Reiki I was competing at a tournament and ended up with an elbow on my shin during a sparring match. Man did that hurt I finished my sparring competition and didn't really notice the pain that much as my adrenaline was so high and I was completely focused on my match. As our matches came to an end, we received our medals and bowed out. I haven't paid much attention to my shin at this time as I was focusing on cheering and supporting my other teammates. I went and changed from my karate Gi to my regular clothes. I had been sitting for a while with one of my friends and fellow teammates as we were watching and supporting our teammates. My friend and I went to get up to move and I had a tough time walking. I could barely put weight on my right leg. My shin was so sore. My friend had to help me out of the tournament. As he and I were leaving with my sensei and his wife (my friends' parents, also my second mom and dad), my head sensei came over and asked me what was wrong. My mom was with my friend and me. I had explained to my head sensei that I had taken an elbow straight on my shin bone in my sparring match. He asked if he could help me. He said he could help to take my pain. I was like "what." He explained Reiki to me. This was my first introduction to Reiki.

He told me that he would put his hand on my shin, I may feel some warmth from the Reiki energy. I was a bit sceptical about it. At this point my shin was throbbing in pain. I was willing to do anything to make the pain stop. As he put his hand on my shin, I noticed he had closed his eyes, and I could feel so much warmth and heat all through my leg. It was an amazing feeling. My head sensei did this for about 30 mins. When he was finished, he asked me to stand up. I was a bit leery. With the help of my friend and my head sensei I was able to get up. I was surprised at how I could now put weight on my leg. My shin was still a bit tender but nowhere near as sore and painful as it was before. This was my first introduction to Reiki and the benefits of Reiki. I was hooked and curious about this Reiki that my head sensei had just performed.

As tradition holds, anytime we had a tournament we would always go for Chinese food. I know it's silly. We compete against each other all day then we go and celebrate with our competitors. It wasn't like a rival between the different clubs, it was more about family and honour. We respected each other and would talk about the tournament and pass on advice to each other. I learned a lot through my 10 years of karate. I learned honour, respect, courage, self esteem. I had a whole other family I looked forward to seeing. Karate also taught me discipline. During my 10 years of karate, I competed in numerous tournaments. I competed in Kata (it's a reenactment of a fight) and Sparring (which is literally wrapping your wrists and putting on the gloves, headgear and a mouth guard and shin pads LOL) and boxing/kickboxing. Most of my winters were spent in a karate dojo and tournaments. I earned numerous medals, I achieved the title C.O.M.A.A (Canadian Open Martial Arts Association) Champion, which means at the end of the tournament season the Association adds up all your points for the year. I earned first place in my division. Through my 10 years I also earned a spot to go to Canadians in Edmonton. This was a huge accomplishment for me. I was really excited about this honour. Karate was a huge part of my life. I am forever grateful for the experience and all I accomplished during my 10 years.

I am a second-degree brown belt in Shotokan Karate. People ask me why I didn't get my black belt. My answer is it's an honour and respect thing. My sensei who had taught me and tested me for all my belts and guided me threw my 10 years of karate retired. To me, I would have wanted him to test me for my black belt. I know it sounds silly, but it wouldn't be the same if another sensei tested me. My sensei helped to mould me to the woman I am today and to have another sensei test me, well to be honest, I would almost feel like that was being disrespectful. Trust me, my sensei has seen me through some good times, rough times and bad times. He always knew when I had a rough day and needed to blow off some steam. I would work on the punching bag for most of the night. I would do kicks and punches and laps. I now know it was stagnant energy that needed to move. To answer everyone's question as to why I didn't get my black belt. It 100% has to do with the very high respect and honour I hold for my sensei.

During my karate training and competitions, I did have time to be a teenager and hang out with my friends. At the age of 15 my friends and I were busy doing what teenage girls do. Talking about boys, makeup, hair and what we will wear to the school dance. Chatting about everywhere we would go when we get our licence and can drive without our parents taking us. A couple friends and I were having a sleepover when one of my friends had just gotten her licence and we had decided to go to the show that was playing in town. As teenagers we were excited that we could actually go somewhere without our parents driving us. At 15 and 16, parents just are not cool in teenagers' eyes.

As we were on our way to the movie (it was March and in Saskatchewan it's still pretty cold and icy) we turned onto a back road. I was familiar with this back road as my grandparents' friends had lived down there all their life and I knew it well. My friend ended up hitting a cattle guard and lost control of the car. I don't really recall all that had happened, I do remember someone told me to duck. I did and as I did, a water irrigation pipe came through the front windshield, and we spun around for like what seemed for hours. The car just wouldn't stop spinning. The back window was smashed out from the pipe, there were shards of glass everywhere. As we finally stopped, we got out of the vehicle and looked back. I am not sure how we made it through that alive.

The car had ended up in a dugout full of water. Thankfully it was still winter, and the water was frozen. We got to the side of the road and a couple of my friends went for help. My friend who was driving was in shock and fell to the ground. I tried to check for a pulse but couldn't find one. I was freaking out. When the ambulance and police got there, they checked as I said I couldn't find one. They did find one and she was okay. My body was still in shock also. If I hadn't ducked when whoever it was, told me to duck, I would have been on the end of that irrigation pipe. My angels were looking out for me that night. As we arrived at the hospital to get checked out, the nurse on duty called all of our parents. Of course, we were all scared about them calling our parents, as we knew we would be in so much trouble (we were not drinking or anything). Surprisingly, our parents were not mad at us. They just hugged us tightly and were glad we were okay. My mom took me home that night. I had her sleep with me as I kept replaying the car accident in my head. My mom was a nurse and I wanted her beside me. For safety, Mom makes everything better with a hug. This would be my second near death experience.

The next couple days were a bit rough and especially trying when we went back to school. As the whole town was talking about it and kids at school were asking what happened. I ran out of a couple of my classes to cry as I couldn't take reliving the whole thing over and over again. I was definitely glad to get home after that day of school. I asked to stay home the next day. I slept. This soon passed and I was able to heal from the trauma of this certain incident. As high school went on, I started dating a guy who I met at one of our high school rodeos. His event was bareback riding. We dated for roughly 3 years. All through high school. I will honestly say he helped my self-worth. He was there to talk to and keep me on track. We eventually broke up as he was still in school, and I was on my way to college. I am grateful we still talk every once in a while, to this day.

As I graduated high school in June 1999, I had planned to take the summer off and just enjoy summer. When fall came it was time for college. I was apprehensive about going and being 4 hours away from my family. I had never been that far away from my family. The most I had been away was a week for summer camps. I was an emotional mess. I had entered the Youth Care Worker program. Let me tell you, that was not what I had expected. I was 19 and struggling. I ended up getting myself into a bit of trouble and headed down the wrong path. I remember this one night in particular, I had been hanging around a not so healthy crowd. They were into drugs and me being from a small town never knew what drugs were. I was like "what weed?" "What's that?" A couple of guys had started to grow it and the cops found out. That night was the scariest night of all. I had found out I was pregnant and then found out that my friends had been growing weed (before it was legal). I was in the back of a cop car. The police had my mom on the phone. I had to make a decision right then and there, be charged with possession of an illegal substance or tell the officer where the weed was and go home to my parents and not come back to this town. I was so scared; I didn't know what was happening. I had never been in trouble with the law ever. I moved home the next day. Mom came to get me. Here I am 19 and expecting. I knew I had to tell my dad about my pregnancy. Another very hard thing to do. My dad hardly talked to me throughout my whole pregnancy. I took that hard. My mom was an amazing support system. The day I had my son in 2000, I never knew what unconditional love was before then. He was perfect in every way.

As time went on, I raised my son and moved a couple of times in 2003 I met a guy. He was every girl's dream, tall, dark and very fit. We dated for a year, and all was good. We got engaged and planned to start a new life together. A couple of months before our wedding I found out I was expecting again. We were so excited about this news. We didn't say anything until after the wedding. We were happy living in wedded bliss. Enjoying being a married couple, until one day when my husband did a complete 360, he became very abusive in every way imaginable. I was so confused and scared. How, did this happen? Why did this happen? I remember the day like it was yesterday. I locked myself and my son who was 5 years old in the bathroom and called my parents to come and get me. They were a few hours away. It took all I had to protect myself, my son and my unborn baby. Knowing my parents were 4 hours away, I was praying that we would still be okay by the time they got there. I was so relieved when I heard my parents' voices outside the bathroom door. What they saw when their daughter unlocked the bathroom door, was heart wrenching. I was 7 months pregnant and black and blue from the neck down. My son was okay. I hadn't felt my unborn baby move in a couple hours. This was not normal, as she was very active. Thankfully my husband left to go to his parents that night and my parents stayed with me. The next day my mom drove me to my doctor to check on the baby as I hadn't felt her move at all. My son and I moved back to my parents' house. I stayed with my parents till my daughter was born in January. The day she was born was yet another scary day. My mom, who was a nurse, came with me when it was time to go. Her labour was extremely hard labour and all in my back. After 7 hours of hard labour my daughter was born. This was not the happy labour a mother looks for. She came out with the cord around her neck, and she had started to turn blue. I had delivered her and then laid back on the delivery table and drifted away. I do remember seeing the bright white lights and feeling so calm and at peace. I wanted to stay there. I heard in the distance, "It's not your time yet, come back to us, it's not your time yet, come back to us." When I did come back, I was so weak. I wanted to get up and stand and see my baby girl. As soon as I stood up, I collapsed to the floor. I was so weak and borderline for a blood transfusion. My new baby girl and I spent a week in the hospital as I had no strength. When we were finally home, I had moved into a family member's trailer in town. The three of us were a happy family. I had the support of my family near me.

A couple of years later. I met my second husband. We were married for 12 years. Our marriage was good in the beginning. We had moved quite a few times in our marriage. It did take a toll on our marriage. During our numerous moves we were trying to add to our family. We had tried for over a year with no luck. We were both getting very discouraged. We finally decided that it wasn't going to happen, and we had quit trying so hard. Shortly after that we got the news we had been waiting for, I was expecting. We were over the moon excited about our new bundle of joy that was joining our family.

This pregnancy was far from easy. I ended up with very high blood pressure and ended up with pre-eclampsia. I had to go every week for a non stress test. I was off work due to my doctor feeling I was on my feet for too many hours a day which wasn't helping myself or my baby. I called my husband and told him that I was feeling lightheaded and dizzy, and I collapsed on the floor as I had no feeling in my legs. His reaction was not the sweetest. He was mad as we would have to go to the hospital yet again and be hooked up to the non stress machine and then sent home. As we had been numerous times prior to this. On this day the doctors couldn't get my blood pressure down at all. When we arrived, they took my blood pressure, and it was 180/190. As my blood pressure did not come down at all, we were faced with another difficult decision. The only way to get my blood pressure down was to deliver the baby. Our un-born baby girl was one month early. As a mom who had two babies prior, I was scared. Every emotion was running through me. I didn't know what to do. The doctor induced me. I had over 5 bags of medication hooked up to my IV pole. I was worried and so scared. I was scared as the baby's lungs may not have been fully developed, I was worried the cord had wrapped around her neck. I didn't know what to do. I was induced and had the epidural. Four hours later my 5-pound 1 ounce baby girl was born. She came out screaming. I wasn't able to see her for long. Just long enough to kiss her little forehead and she was on her way to NICU. That was music to my ears as I knew her lungs had developed. I could see the nurse's facial expressions all through her delivery. They were very worried. I had asked the nurse after my daughter was moved to NICU "how bad was it?" She said, "it wasn't good." I said "please just give it to me straight. My mom is a nurse, and she has always been straight forward with me about medical things." I said, "I can "handle it." My nurse looked at me with relief in her eyes and said, "sweetie if you had waited another 24 hours it would not have been good, decisions would have had to be made, tough decisions." I spent a couple days in the hospital. Then I was faced with another hurdle. She had to stay in NICU as her sucking reflex wasn't fully developed. I had to leave my brand-new baby girl in the hospital till she was able to keep her milk down. I cried as I had never had to leave any of my babies at the hospital before. They came home with me. She spent 12 days in NICU and was released the day of my birthday. One birthday I will never forget.

As we started our new life with the five of us, we again moved a couple times. It took a toll on us. My husband started to grow very distant. Again, I was asking myself "why." We were blessed by a surprise two year later. We were expecting again. We were both shocked and surprised as we hadn't really been talking about another baby. He was definitely a surprise. My blood pressure had started to go up again. My doctor had watched my blood pressure all through this pregnancy. Halloween came and my blood pressure kept going up, off to the doctor I went. The nurses and doctor monitored my blood pressure, and it wasn't staying stable. It would go up and down. My doctor finally said it's time to go to the emergency room. Another ambulance ride and we were on our way. My doctor was in the ambulance with me. He never rides in the ambulance unless it is very serious. I have never seen my doctor so worried in all the years I had been seeing him. He had the shot in his pocket if things turned for the worse. As, we arrived at the emergency room, my doctor came with me everywhere. My husband was somewhere. I was hooked up to the non-stress machine and my blood pressure was still going up and down. When the nurse came in, she explained to me that I could possibly go back home and wait another week. I looked at my husband and we both decided no. We explained to him what happened with our daughter previously and we didn't want to go through that again. The nurse went and expressed our concerns to the emergency doctor. She had agreed with our decision. I was induced shortly after that, and my son arrived six hours later. When he came into the world and the nurse had said "he isn't crying" those are three words a mom who has just delivered doesn't want to hear. I panicked. My husband assured me he was ok. As a mom you need to hear that cry. He did eventually. I felt a sense of relief. We spent four days in the hospital and got to go home.

A few months after my son was born, my husband began to grow distant. I found myself asking "why" again. We had moved back to Ontario, and he was never there. He always had to work late and never wanted to do anything. As a few years past we found ourselves in a pandemic. This was when reality set in. My husband was never there. He was always on his phone, going to the garage or outside, and going for drives. He had turned cold. I suffered from every abuse possible from him and I didn't know why? My constant wondering was taking a toll on me. I had no emotion, no feelings, he had stripped me of everything. One day I found out why he had been messaging another woman. They had been planning their wedding and were planning to take my kids away. I hit rock bottom. I felt 100 knives to my heart. I was heartbroken. He was in the shower and as I read the messages I collapsed to the floor. My kids were home as we were in the beginning of a pandemic. I ran out to the garage with a knife and slit my wrist. I was devastated. As I saw the blood run down my wrist, I cried and cried. What had I done? How could I do this to my kids and leave them without their mom. My, husband came out and saw what I had done. For the first time in a long time, I saw some remorse for what he had put me through. I went to the bathroom, and he helped me to wrap my wrist.

Then the verbal abuse started again. I had enough. Luckily, he went to work after that I called my healthcare provider, and she was on the phone with me in seconds. I explained to her what had happened and that I needed help. We got me on medication and signed up for a waitlist for a psychiatrist. As I waited for the call for an appointment from a psychiatrist, I spoke with a social worker weekly. She and I had recommended a plan for me and the kids to get out of this unhealthy situation.

The Friday of the May long weekend 2020 I packed myself and my kids and what all we were able to fit in my SUV and we left after my husband had gone to work. We lived in a motel for a couple months till I was able to find an apartment. I had notified the police as to what was happening as I knew my husband would have called the police on me for leaving with the kids. Sure, enough he did. The police came to see me at the motel to do a wellness check to be sure that the kids and I were okay. They red flagged him so he couldn't leave the province or the country with the kids. The police told him if he showed up at the motel he would be charged. As the pandemic continued, we went through the courts. He made it as difficult as he could. We eventually came to agreements. During this process I also started to find my voice again. I found me.

As I found myself and healed, I started my healing process by signing up for a Reiki Level I and II Course which a co-worker (whom we ended up being good friends) had suggested to me as she had done a couple of women' circles with the Reiki Teacher. I looked up the Reiki teacher and found she was offering a course. I signed up. I learned so much in my two-day course. I healed some past wounds and found myself again. The girl I knew I was. As I went through my Level I and II! I met an amazing group of women who also had started their healing journey. We laughed, we cried, and we held space for each other as we were all starting our own healing journeys. We were a tribe for the week-end. As our weekend came to a close and we all passed our Reiki Level I and II, we learned that our teacher was going to do a Reiki Master course in the spring. Me being me and having experienced Reiki and its healing benefits at a very young age and always curious about it, I signed up to take my Reiki Masters. My Reiki Masters was very up lifting. I learned so much. I did so much healing at my Master class. I was with another group of amazing people. I got a glimpse of a couple of my past lives. One being ancient Egyptian. I under-stood why ancient Egypt was so interesting and empowering to me as a stu-dent in school learning about the Egyptians. I was on a different level and was awakened by so much. During this Master class, I learned about a new Reiki Masters course that was going to be coming up, this was Karuna Reiki Mas-ters. More, Reiki and more levelling up. Absolutely sign me up for this. I did. This was another empowering course as this one in particular was working with The Divine Feminine. This one was so empowering. I learned so much about myself and my Divine Feminine self. In the first year of the pandemic, I became a double Reiki Master and was practising Reiki regularly. I had found my pur-pose in this life as I had wondered so often about. I have embraced my healing path with Reiki. I never thought at my karate tournament, when my head sensei first introduced me to Reiki, that it was part of my path, my story. The empowerment I have embraced from my Reiki trainings has changed my life completely.

As I started on my soul's journey, I have been introduced to so many other people who are on this path also. I met a Results Coach, and she introduced me to hypnotherapy. I had always wondered about hypnosis. No not the stage kind where they make you walk around and cluck like a chicken. The hypnosis that heals past traumas, emotions and well being. I signed up for a break-through coaching session with her. Wow I was so surprised at the emotions and traumas that came up, I thought I had healed from many of them; however, they were partially healed but not all the way. This was on a whole new level. She was also an NLP (Neuro Linguistic Practitioner) Coach, she and I worked on healing what was ready to be healed. I learned about my unconscious mind. Well, this sparked my attention, lit a fire in me that I wanted to go and get. You bet I did. I finished my 10-week breakthrough coaching session and wanted more. I knew I was definitely following my soul's calling now. When I learned about a Hypnosis course coming up, I signed up for it, ASAP. I knew then and there I wanted to help and guide others just as my coach had helped and guided me. She showed me how to look within myself and love myself. I wanted to learn how and why and where was all this when I was in school. I wanted to share the amazing news about how I grew into the woman I was always meant to be. I did my hypnosis course in November of 2021 and have just recently finished my own NLP course. My NLP course was very intense. I brought up stuff about me. How my behaviours and strategies were needing an upgrade. No, this course did not come lightly. I had my red-hot mess moments and my give up moments. Through my Hypnosis and NLP training I have learned so much and become so empowered with all I can do and am supposed to do. My conscious and unconscious mind are working together.

I am extremely excited and very proud to share with everyone that yes it may feel like you are in the mud all the time and yes it sucks. Remember the lotus flower always emerges from the mud and muck, shining and looking so beautiful. I have been through my fair share of mud and muck, and I have emerged as the lotus flower. There is a light at the end of the tunnel. You are all magnificent and have so much to share with the world. Let your light shine as bright as the morning sun. There is always help for you. I am proud to say, I have been through this journey, I have had the hurricane come, I have hit rock bottom, I have grown, and I have healed. I am on my journey to Happy, Healthy and Wealthy. I have spent the pandemic working on myself and healing myself.

Self-Love is key.

DEDICATION

I dedicate this book to my mother. You have always been there for me and guided me with words of wisdom and your faith in me. My kids have shown me and helped me to become the mother and woman I am today. My best friend who has always been there for me and seen me threw my ups and downs. They are my biggest cheerleaders. I love you all so much.

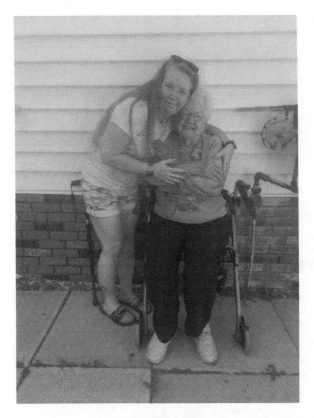

Here's me and my Grandmother she was 98 and passed
Away the day before my birthday.

Accept what is,
let go of what
was, and have
faith in what
will be

My 2018 at a Glance

By Judy Gaw

I am writing this to give you all HOPE! My very soul: Since the Stroke in 2018!

For 10 plus years I have written, from my heart, a daily gratitude journal to document the blessings that I am grateful for. I have always believed that I am an extremely grateful person for anything I have ever had, such as, my love for God, my husband, my family, my friends, my church family, my forever family (Celebrate Recovery), good deeds, blessings, gifts, etc.

However, since the stroke, it is so profound now. I have such a deeper appreciation for every person, every visit, every phone call, and every text (once I learned to read again) after being in a vegetative state for 6 to 7 days and my husband, feeling it was the end of life as we knew it. Hearing my care pastor, Donna Moss, praying over me. God was right there with us; I heard every word she said to me God is with us.

I am even grateful for the hallucinations of the bugs crawling all over me, one of the nurses washed my hair pulling it all out, etc. Learning how to walk and talk, struggling with stuttering, reading and writing, thankfully, I use my microphone to make words. Learning how to make change for the parking meter, making a cherry cheesecake and a chicken and stuffing casserole, while I was in rehab, to my fears of too many people coming at me all at once. All my hard work is paying off I am blessed beyond measures.

It is a different kind of appreciation that I've never had before. My special friends who came to visit me every day and take me to my appointments to enticing me to go out for dinner to give Hugh a break. Remembering how to drive and the confidence to drive again with my friends trusting that I could do it. I have the best friends ever! People have told me I am a "Walking Miracle!"

Triple A Surgery! April 20, 2018

I am dedicating this chapter of my life to my Lord and Saviour, Jesus Christ. Praise be to God. The day has finally arrived! I am so excited for this to be all over. The waiting game is always brutal! I got a date to go into St. Michael's hospital for the abdominal aorta aneurysm (Triple-A) on April 20th, 2018. I was to go into the hospital the day before, to get me all set up. When I arrived at my semi-private room, I was shocked to see my roommate was a man! Holy hell. I went into a full out panic attack. I could not breathe. I wrote on Facebook how upset I was, and my friends started pouring out prayers, Reiki and wise words. One of the pastors at my church told my care pastor Donna Moss about this situation and she called me straight away. Donna calmed me down and immediately started laughing at what we were saying.

My son was here for a couple of days in 2022, he was the final piece of the puzzle on what happened that day. 9 hours later! Finally, I had the full picture from Hugh, Devin and Joyce of that day and the seven days in ICU. From my early days when Hugh thought that I was going to be a vegetable the rest of my life, to the growth leaps and bounds into an even better life than I had had before! I did, however, remember being in a St. Michael's hospital bed and my very good friend Barb visiting along with Mel and Shirley! I saw this bald man who scared me so bad that apparently my feet were pushed on my bed to make me go farther and farther and farther away from him. Hugh kept saying, "Judy it's OK...Judy calm down, it's ok, it's Mel...Judy it's Mel and Shirley, you know them!" Hearing all those words in my brain I remembered them and remembered they were safe and that I was safe to be with them. What I really remember is Mel asking if it was ok for them to say the Serenity Prayer before they left. I said yes, the only way I knew how at that time apparently, was with a grunt. So, I think you get the picture, eh? When Mel started to say it and I said it word for word out loud, that was a huge WOW for me. I didn't know I Could talk.

My journey continued, with me going to Providence Villa in Toronto. To start, I learned to walk and talk and chew gum as the saying goes. Oh my, I remember they made me walk up and down the stairs. I was in excruciating pain. I didn't know how to do it. I learned quickly enough, didn't I. After a month I went home, and the wait began to get Physiotherapy, Speech Therapy and Occupational Therapy. I think it took about 3 months before I was able to do those things at Lakeridge Health Centre in Whitby, Ontario. The first thing I instinctively knew how to do, was make a pot of coffee! I had no idea how to cook or anything, however, I knew how to make that pot of coffee. Yay me! I remember learning how to put coins in a parking machine so that I wouldn't get a ticket. Barb taught me how to count the coins to make sure I did it correctly and then I could do it by myself. That in and of itself was a miracle for me. There I also learned all the in-between stuff, to me doing multiple courses. I am learning leaps and bounds, to where my ultimate goal is to better the lives of others from trauma to suicide and everything in between. I am well on my way to being where God wants me to be.

Thank You, Jesus! Amen.

April 20, 2019

I am grateful that I had friends such as Joyce Deschamps, Barbara Johnstone, Lynn Milne and Diane Marven, which were there to take good care of me every step of the way. Let's not forget about the many hospital and home visits with Robert Fraser, Mel and Shirley Bushby. I learned to talk again without stuttering … unless my brain is really tired! I learned to put coins in a parking metre so that I could pay for my parking. I worked very closely with my physiotherapist, my speech therapist and my occupational therapist to which I exceeded their expectations of me! My speech therapist told me that I've been doing really well at finding different words when I'm speaking gibberish.

I am absolutely thrilled to see my progress!

I have learned how to read again, write again, walk again (300 steps), I have learned to count from 1 to 100, to cook some things! I am still learning! Of course, it really helps when you get an instant pot and an air fryer! The biggest thing is that I am driving my SUV again! Oh, and I can dance again! I'm pretty good at taking my medication every day! I am very proud of the progress that I have made. Actually, I'm thrilled! I'm excited to see how many more accomplishments I'll be making. God Bless.

Thank Goodness for my Microphone!

October 26, 2019, I became second Degree Level REIKI Practitioner!

In October 2020 we sold our home of 26 years in Pickering Ontario and purchased our new home two hours and 30 minutes away from my friends, on January 27th, 2021. It was very difficult moving and being alone. I really struggled with the move and not knowing anyone I was so alone! Friends told me they were coming to visit. Wrong! Nobody came except David and Zelda for their 40th wedding anniversary. It was a surprise.

YAY GOD!

Time was going by and still no one! I was done! The very evening, I had everything ready to end it all and my girlfriend Geri phoned. I answered and when she asked how I was, I said fine, then I yelled "I'm NOT FINE." I'm having suicidal thoughts. I blurted everything out! When I was finished Geri said, "that's why I'm calling. I told you I would come before the snow flew and that is why I'm calling.

How does next weekend sound?" I'm like yes, yes, YES! You see that gave me hope.

I signed up for an eCPR course, which I passed and as of February 20, 2022, I am now an eCPR Practitioner! I have not had any suicidal thoughts in the last 5 years Anniversary-April 20, 2023.

I AM ANEURYSM FREE!!!

I am screaming from the Mountain Tops…. Woohoo! My vascular surgeon called me today to give me the great news! Needless, to say, I am ecstatic! I have cried today with so much joy and happiness! These are a few of my accomplishments over the last five years!

I am running my Health and Wellness Business again!

DEDICATION

My Father Daddy, Jesus, Holy Spirit, My Loving Husband Hugh. My incredible amazing son Devin, and sweetheart of a Daughter-In-law Tammy. My gorgeous grandchildren Justin, Ethan and (Miss. Rosie) Jessica. Also, my beautiful gorgeous daughter, Amy. Best Friends, Rob, Joyce and Barb. Thank you, Lord for all my blessings!

Me Today

My loving husband and I

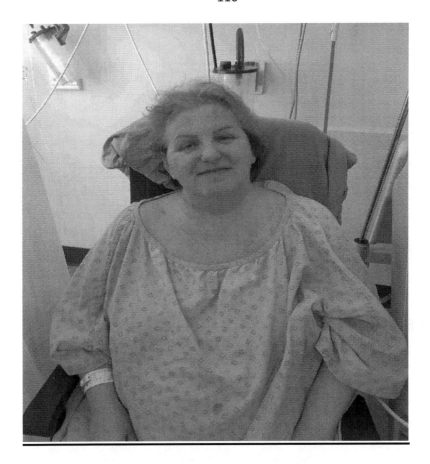

Where I was 6 years ago

Be proud of every step you take ! It got you to where you are today!

Www.empoweredinheels.org

Beyond The Edge
By Judy Swallow

I cannot say I have ever been empowered in heels, but I have been empowered in figure skates almost my whole life. I began skating at the age of 4 and skated for 15 to 20 hours a week from the ages of 9 to 17. I then coached from the age of 18 to 59. Suffice to say I spent a great deal of time on the ice with skates tied to my feet.

I loved skating. I had a natural talent that easily kept me interested in wanting to learn and do more. It was also a great deal of fun to skate with others who became close friends and gave support through the more challenging moments of tests failed and competitions that didn't go as planned. Participating in bi-annual ice shows, was a blast. Learning show numbers without the pressure of training too hard are cherished memories. On the coaching side, ice shows were a big production and entailed a great deal of "behind the scenes" work, but easy to do when the kids enjoyed performing so much for the audiences.

As much as I love skating and enjoyed coaching, and as empowering as wearing my skates did feel, I have to admit it was not my dream work. Coaching did give me amazing opportunities and experiences, including coaching in both Denmark and Sweden for several years. I travelled extensively during that time, visiting many other European countries, and even had a dream trip of trekking the Himalayas in Nepal. Prior to this I had travelled only to Florida and Texas because my parents were living there, and that was it. I also changed and grew in ways that only living on my own, in a new country could provide.

Besides skating, from a young age I was also very curious about what makes people ticks.

When I was 8 years old, I was standing on the bottom landing of the stairway in our house, my sister was half way up the stairs and could still see into the living room where our parents were seated. I had no idea what was going on but she was yelling at them, almost in a rage. I looked up at her and for a moment, I was totally detached from the situation. I showed no emotion, I had no fear, I was simply a spectator. The more I watched, the more I began to question: "What makes people tick?" I was so mesmerized by their interaction and behaviour. This triggered something inside of me that grew over the years.

In my teenage years I became very interested in creative visualization and the mental aspects of being an athlete. So much so I was intent on going to university to become a sport psychologist. Which, I did go to university but what I was learning was not what I was seeking, except for one course I took in my third year: "Mystical Teachings in Science and Psychology." I felt I had come home. I found what I was looking for. Consciousness! This course was about ancient and mystical teachings in human consciousness, the soul, the psyche and looking IN to the self. All the other courses I was taking were dry, theoretical and filled with oppositional ideas about the mind, brain, and human behaviour. I couldn't stand the psychology program and I didn't think I could study consciousness in an academic setting like university, so I got my Bachelor of Arts degree and got out.

During these young adult years, I also began to ask myself some deeper existential questions. Away from work, my university courses, friends, and family, I was really beginning to wonder, "Why am I here? What is the purpose of life? Who am I? What am I?" and in my solitude, I admitted a number of "truths" I had.

The first thing I admitted was I was not truly happy. I knew deep within myself that life was meant to be joyful and it was feeling anything but this way. Yes, I was enjoying going out with friends, enjoying coaching, being able to pay for my car and rent, but there was an emptiness to this too. I struggled with feeling good enough as a coach, comparing myself to others. I struggled with relationships and almost always being attracted to the wrong guys, ending up with a broken heart more times than I care to count. I simply didn't feel good enough or confident in my own skin.

.

A lot of this was due to the fact that as much as I loved skating itself, there were aspects to it that shot down my self-esteem. I was talented, so it was natural that I would skate competitively, but being competitive was not really in my DNA. I so admire athletes that love to compete. I never loved to compete, so doing so was a chore, and then being judged, compared, and ranked, took a toll on me emotionally, and was still impacting me as a young   adult.

My family life was also a combination of being well provided for and yet emotionally unstable. My father was a "functioning alcoholic." I was never sure if "mad dad" or "happy dad" would show up when he drank. Now I can look back and see that his stress about not having enough money would trigger "mad dad" but at the time I would just hope it would be a happy night in the house. When it was not, the yelling and fighting between my parents was terrifying. It was also confusing for my young mind to square his financial stress with all that he provided, from skating lessons, to a trailer and boat for our summers, plenty of food to eat, and a home to lay our heads at night. I never quite understood my dad's financial "state", but I do believe that it was connected to his self-worth and self-value, and I inherited a similar state.

I suppose growing up in and of itself is just simply tumultuous. Kids can be cruel, and at the time when I was young, emotional well-being was not really on the radar of society as a whole. Teachers, parents, coaches, all did their best, but I don't recall being asked how, or what I felt in different situations and how it was impacting my well-being. We just got on with getting on. Cry it out in private, keep the pain to myself, is really what I learned to do.

It was these life experiences that became the impetus to answer those existential questions, the desire to be happy in my skin, to feel self-worth, and the true joy I knew life was meant to be.

I have never seen myself as an entrepreneur in the traditional sense, nor do feel I have those qualities associated with it but I have to say that I do feel I am an "Entrepreneur of the Soul." The seeking, the yearning to know who and what I am, what makes human beings tick, why I am here, why any of us are here, became my mission and was, and is, my true passion. Inner work was my work, and it is where I would put my energy and focus when I wasn't at my job. Everything else, including making money, was secondary. I have always had enough money, sometimes barely enough but I knew that I had to seek and find the answers to these questions.

During these decades of seeking and focusing on my inner self, one of my choices was to enrol in a three-year psychotherapy training program at the Transpersonal Therapy Center in Toronto. This was one year after I returned from Sweden and finally feeling "grounded" back in Canada again.

Nearing the end of the first year of training, we had an associate teacher come to facilitate our weekend-long class. We did one of these each month to be able to go more in-depth into different training modalities and our own processes. This particular teacher specialized in Shamanistic Psychotherapy. The final process he was doing for the weekend was a "Threshold Guided Meditation." I had mentioned prior to it happening that there was a deep sadness in me that no matter what I did, I could not get rid of. His reply to this was simply, "You're ripe."

We began the meditation and while speaking, he was rhythmically drumming. I felt very safe and very surrendered to the process. When he guided us to see a room before us, with people in there and then to step across the threshold of the door into the room. I was instantly aware of my muscles beginning to twitch and before I knew it, I was kicking and screaming at the top my lungs, for my mommy and daddy to come get him off of me. I was a toddler again and I was being "attacked." It was real and visceral, and I was making such a commotion that he had to stop the meditation. Others in the group had their process disturbed, but I could not help it. I was re-experiencing a molestation that was buried deep in my psyche   and   body.

I was brought back to being aware of the room, group, present moment and was given the space to just sit, and not continue on with the process. I was fortunate to be in a safe, loving "container" and this teacher made sure I was okay before I needed to head home.

So, deep within, I was ripe and ready for this breakthrough that was so integral to the transformation of my self-confidence and self-image. The healing I needed to continue to do once I had this memory retrieval, was extensive. There were many "tentacles" to it, but I can honestly say that through my tenacity, and the support I had from wise teachers, I forgave the person who did this and I expunged the experience from my body and psyche. A clear indication of this, was that I had experienced night terrors during my childhood and into my adult years. I would wake up anybody who was in the vicinity when I had one of these "dreams." They were always the same. I would be screaming at the top of my lungs to be helped to get someone off of me. My heart would be racing and most times I jumped out of the bed and that was when I would wake up. After more than 3 decades, they came to an end after this healing.

Many of the night terrors are "memorable," but one time in particular was both embarrassing and funny. I was on a solo. two-week vacation in the United Kingdom. I bought a rail pass and travelled to different parts of the

England, Scotland and Wales, staying in hostels or camping. When I arrived on the Isle of Skye in northern Scotland, it was dark and rainy. There was just one hostel and it was filled up that night. Yes, I had a night terror and as usual, I was screaming and jumped out of the bed. Word got around by breakfast time that it was me, and though I apologized, it wasn't needed. Everyone was kind and understanding.

Every workshop, lecture, course, or retreat I attended, and every book I read, was worth it, because in the "end, " I feel like a billionaire.

Going within, and cultivating a self-awareness which revealed a deep level of self-loathing, shame, wounding, and lack of self-worth is priceless. It's painful and it's difficult but it pays off in spades to be living a life wherein I have the skills, tools and abilities to transform negative and fear-based consciousness into Love. Self-love, self-worth, self-esteem and an ever expanding self-image, that I am so powerful, creative, dynamic and beautiful than I was ever taught.

In essence, self-loathing was transmuted into self-love over those decades. It was a lot of three steps forward, two steps back, traversing through the emotional, mental, and spiritual landscapes of ME. There wasn't an easy way to get through the depths of shame, anger, unworthiness, and unconscious self-loathing and limiting beliefs I held about myself, my parents, the world, and God. I am a firm believer that if you call out in earnest to be "saved," your life will fall apart even more. A total breakdown, to be able to breakthrough. It was tough love coming from "above" but there was no other way. The truth and power of who and what human beings really are, is not handed to us on a silver platter. If it was, we would still not see our true value nor the gift that life is and the gift that each of us is.

I had imagined that once I found the answers to the existential questions, healed many deep wounds, trauma and felt I had the tools to navigate life's ups and downs, I would then just coast and enjoy life to the end of my days, but what happened next showed me that I was very much mistaken.

I had not been in a relationship for close to 5 years when I earnestly felt that I was ready to be in one. There is a saying, "Be careful what you wish for."

I received that relationship and for the past nine years I have changed in ways I couldn't have imagined because this man is a "conspiracy theorist." He and I often butted heads in the early stages of our relationship because I couldn't believe the information that he was wanting me to look at was even remotely true.

However, being in relationship meant to me to at least look at what he is saying before outright denying its possibility. Like I did with my personal life, I went deep into areas I had not explored or even known about. It was another experience of the nesting "Russian Dolls." Personally, I had kept revealing deeper layers of myself that I needed to look at through those many years, and the same was now happening with society at large.

I began looking at news and information that was painting a different picture and perspective on life as I knew it; that there were things out of my personal control that impacted my life. I was beginning to see a bigger system   at   play.

Questions started to emerge again, similar but different to the ones I asked over 30 years earlier.

What if we are way more than we have ever been led to believe?

What if the concept and image we hold of ourselves as humans is just a fraction of what is true?

What if there was a concerted effort by just a few beings, compared to the masses, that have a vested interest in keeping humanity from knowing the Truth about Itself, and our history?

What if those which are deemed "Conspiracy Theories" are more accurate accounts of the events that go on?

What if the following statement is true?

"In January 1967...the CIA published a memo to all its stations, suggesting the use of the term "conspiracy theorists" for everyone criticizing the Warren Report findings. Until then the press and the public mostly used the term "assassination theories" ...[But] with this memo this changed and very soon "conspiracy theories" became what it is until today: a term to smear, denounce and defame anyone who dares to speak about any crime committed by the state, military or intelligence services." Martain Broeckers, author of JFK: Coup D'Etat in Americas"

 Off I dove down into the proverbial rabbit hole. The internet was a bastion of information. A small sample of what I learned: where money comes from and how central banks work, about geopolitics, war, and what a false flag is; I learned of a man named Nikola Tesla and his work in free energy, and a topic I least expected to engage with, the possibility if Extra-Terrestrial Life; thar we are not alone in this vast Universe.

I sincerely began questioning what I thought I knew.

As difficult as it was to believe, the following made more to sense me than anything I was told by teachers of the media.

"Lies have always been used to sell war to a public that would otherwise be leery about sending their sons off to fight and die on foreign soil... [In] the modern age of democracy and volunteer armies, a pre-tense for war is required to rally the nation around the flag and motivate the public to fight....[From] false flag attacks to dehumanization of the "enemy,"....[Throughout] the last century, a host of methods have been employed to keep the public playing the military-industrial complex's game." James Corbett, Debunking a Century of Wars

I mean surely, we as humans could come up with the skills to negotiate peace with fellow humans, so deliberate war games for a barrage of reasons, became possible to me.

I also found the following idea, put forth by Lisa Renee- the founder of Energetic Synthesis, very fascinating: "We are a race of people that are purposely hypnotized by survival and poverty consciousness....The medical system does not want us healthy and well, as they profit when we're sick... The banking system does not want us to be out of debt or interest obligation because we are easier to control when we are in debt."

I had learned banks make their money through debt so, again, this was making sense and somewhat answering my questions, "Why do I have to work so hard to pay for the basics of life; food, shelter, clothing, education and medicine? Why are these monetized?" And, "Is the epitome of human existence to be consumers?

I couldn't help but ask: What if there is an actual agenda to keep us believing and feeling that human suffering is just the way it has to be?

For me, this is not only possible, it has become probable that there is a concerted, very organized effort by a few to control the many.

It is the most unexpected change in my life: to be a "conspiracy theorist" though I would still call my self a "Truth Seeker." With my previous personal transformation, and now the shift in my perspective on how the world Possibly works, I have to ask, What if Human suffering is NOT the Way it has to be?

What if the Truth is, we are actually Infinite Beings of Love, Light, and Power?

What if we are the Power and Love that can bring in the "Golden Age" we hope for in our Hearts?

What if Paradise depends on us being courageous and facing the big and powerful Oz and finding out what Dorothy did; that it's just a weak, old man hiding behind a curtain?

Paradise. The Golden Age. What if this is what we are here to create?

Now that I have arrived at the conviction that we have been manipulated to think and believe, in certain ways; that propaganda is a tool for control to affect how we see the world and the events that take place, to keep us in a frequency of fear, I am more empowered than I have ever been to bring to light our true and magnificent nature. I am a warrior of love in this proverbial battle between light and dark, be it within the self or within the collective.

What's happened in the past 3 years due to covid, has magnified my seeing this time in history as a profound battle for humanity's freedom and evolution versus becoming more enslaved to systems of control.

Like so many others who wanted body autonomy and freedom of choice, I lost my job and income. I found it incredible that I was forced to make this choice between "a jab or a job." But, it was an easy choice because I had not trusted mainstream media and the government for years, and I was clear I would not be coerced into something I was very wary of. It took decades for me to value myself and to be able to stand in my power, and this was a magnificent test of my commitment to myself. I wasn't going to succumb to the fear that was being pushed onto all of us. I had no judgement toward those who chose to take the vaccination, or felt it was the only choice they could make because of finances. What an awful position to be in and my heart truly went out to these people. No one should ever be put in this position in a free society. What was difficult, was the division that was fomented between people, and fear won out over compassion in a big way.

I know I was angry at people for not considering they have been hoodwinked and lied to. Some of my family and friends were angry at me for my viewpoints. It was messy, yet I don't believe anyone had any true ill-intent in their heart. I know I did not, and I do not.

All of this was something I had to navigate through. Balancing self-love and my love for family and friends who stood on the other side of the fence. I really did not see this coming as an outcome of that which began in March of 2020, but it is, and another surprise is what a gift it has been.

The gift has been to go through a further letting go of the past. Who I was in relationship to work, money, friends and family, was up again for further transformation. One of the most trying situations was, and is, with my dear sister. She is a few years older than me, and throughout our childhood and beyond, she's always had my back. We were close. We both skated, I skated because of her. She wanted to learn to skate so badly, and I was taken along to the rink to do the same. At one point, she even became my coach. I was her Maid of Honour when she got married. For a number of years, we coached at the same club, after I returned from Sweden. She was also on a spiritual journey as she got older, and we could share about life on some pretty deep levels at times.

We were also very different, and it was the covid situation that brought this into stark light. The differences were beginning to show themselves prior to this time because I was so gung-ho about all these discoveries I was making about the world not being as I once believed it to be. That is, that our government, media, banking and corporations, were trustworthy in any way, shape or form. Our conversations would get intense. I wanted her to hear me, she did not want to hear what I had to say. We began to acknowledge that skating was our glue, and a lovely glue at that, but that our lives were quite divergent and been so for a very long time. She dreamt of being married and having kids, I did not. She was certain she wanted to coach skating, I was not. She did get married and had three children, and lived in one home for her most of her adult life. I stayed single, moved every year or two, dove deep into a spiritual journey and moved out of the country for a while, but none of this caused any big fissures until covid came.

This is when the "big sister-little sister" dynamic was now going to be broken open. This dynamic was not "conscious" for either of us until it was so apparent I was still wanting her approval on some level, and she no longer wanted to take care of me emotionally, as she had our entire lives. Covid and our different viewpoints on it became the talking points, or more apt, arguing points, of this greater shift taking place: freeing myself from this ingrown dynamic and thus, freeing myself to be myself. I wanted to be free of self-censoring because I might upset her, and I imagine she needed freedom from me because my viewpoints were so unaligned with her and her family. It was just not going to work to really be in contact with each other.

This was difficult on our mother, as she wanted there to be peace between us, but she also eventually surrendered and realized we needed our space to process and live life the way we each needed to, without the pressure of "we shuld be at peace because we are sisters."

The situation with her brought such a rich opportunity to "be love". Back tracking a bit here, I was out on a date with someone I had just met in 2012. We were just doing the usual chit-chat and I was saying that I enjoyed coaching but still thought about doing other things. Then he asked me, "What do you want to be?" I sat there for a moment, and then I said to this man I just met, "I want to be love." It was out of my mouth before I could even wonder if he would think this to be a rather weird response.

So, here I am, 11 years later, and I really see the past decade as granting me this wish. Being love in a way that transcends my self-image, the identities, and the roles I play, to stand in the freedom of who I am, and release myself from the fear, conditioning, and programming I grew up with.

Who taught me to be me? Who taught me to see, think and believe what I did about myself and the world? Did I choose or was I told what to choose, guided by lines already drawn out on the path we call life?

I really began to think, without resentment, that it has been the blind leading the blind for generations now. Many of us have just done what was modelled for us to do. No matter how well intentioned parents, teachers, and society itself are, I don't think we really question for long enough why we do what we do. I also suppose it was the age old belief that a baby is born as an empty slate and needs to be taught everything rather than nurtured and guided to realize its own brilliance and innate abilities. Sometimes it is a great fit for a person and they feel joy, safety, and contentment with the "model" and thrive within it. For others, the "rebels" and "black sheep", perhaps it feels like a straight jacket and their soul is restless. Either way, being taught or shown to truly love yourself was not on the radar screen, or maybe just a hokey idea and unworthy of consideration.

I believe now, I couldn't be love because I really wasn't taught how to love myself. Without self-love, love is not complete. And that is really what I have been working on for decades now, and especially the most recent one. I believe if we can treat ourself the way we want to be treated, not just treat others the way we want to be treated, we would alleviate a great amount of neediness and looking to others to fulfill us in some way. We would have a metaphorical full cup that we can give from, rather than seeking out others to fill it for us. We can continually fill it from the inside, and joyously share, and joyously receive.

My sister and her family, and a few other friends who have become more distant, are teaching me to stand in the power of love for myself, and at the same time, showing me that I must mature, to let them go and be exactly who they want and need to be. That was the sticky part of me that did not want to let go. The part of me that needed them to approve of and acknowledge what I was saying. This was my inner child that lives on no matter how old I get. Sometimes she is divine, and other times, a down right brat. Sometimes so fearful, I am awake at 3 am worrying about everything; sometimes "she" is cracking a joke and I am laughing out loud at my own silliness. But, the one thing I must be aware of is that this "inner child energy" does not hijack my psyche any more. That is, becoming like a needy child wanting what she wants, when she wants, and I am reacting to people or situations from this energy.

Self-love does not mean giving yourself permission to act anyway you want to. Love Encapsulated respect, care, compassion and affection.

Actually, every relationship, and all different kinds of circumstances are golden in giving me the chance to choose love over fear. Which in essence, this all boils down to, I know I am no saint and I get angry, curse, and whine with the best of them, but the gift of seeing how much I need to continue to let go to be love is priceless. I will be coming back to this over and over and over again. Maybe there will be one day I will be standing in the purity of love for myself and all others, with a smile from ear to ear and this is my natural state of being, but until then, I must remain diligent in making sure I am not reacting to people and circumstances with neediness or anger. I know life will not disappoint me in giving me every chance to achieve this.

With even more pressure from outside forces to accept a digital world, and hook up to devices and the Internet of "Things," I am feeling the warrior in me being activated in ever greater amounts. The "Entrepreneur of the Soul" that I considered myself to be, could now also be called a Warrior for Love. There is no contradiction in being a warrior for love, as it is similar to righteous anger. The digitalization of human beings is the antithesis to freedom. We were born free and we have lost sight of this, to the point now where we have totally forgotten that the government is in place to serve us; they are our public servants, but now they are dictating to us what we are to do. Sleight of hand. So clever most of us have not noticed.

I have, and I am on fire about it. This fire has continued to burn up any and all deeper misconceptions about myself and being able to take on such a Goliath as the government and its cronies. The thing I have going for me is, I can look straight into the pit of darkness, sometimes called evil, and I am not afraid of it. Now.

I was afraid before, but I am not now because I have been cleansed of my fear of death. Once this happened, there is nothing out there that can have power over me. I can hold both light and dark. I don't need to deny looking at the negative because it is scary, as I am becoming a greater being of love. Losing what I have in the past three years has given me this.

When I say I will take on the government, "Goliath", I mean, I am saying no to whatever they tell me I need to do. I am living only as an outward expression of my true inner light and freedom. Doing otherwise is a death greater than losing my body to physical death. I don't mean this to sound dramatic, if it does it is simply my being empowered in heels, or running shoes,   or   sandals,   or   barefoot.

It's now a few weeks since I finished writing up to this point. I have been unsure what more, if anything, I would like to give voice to. So, I am deciding to do a "morning papers" process.

This exercise is from a book by Julia Cameron, "The Artist's Way." I bought this book while living in Sweden, and I still bring myself back to it when I am unsure about what I want to write but want to get the "creative juices" flowing. Basically, the process is to commit to writing 3 pages upon awakening. Write whatever it is that's on your mind, even if it's, "I don't know what to write", for 3 pages. No editing of thoughts or words is allowed. Free flow. I was always surprised by where I would begin, emotionally and mentally, and where I would end up, after the 3 pages were done. So, here it goes: June 9, 2023

Happy Friday! Weather is rainy today so I am glad to be home and snuggled up in my bed, writing this for "Empowered In Heels 3." I have been putting off getting to it again because I did not know what to write and I am still short on how long it needs to be. Haha, I am editing. Stop it, Judy! Yeah, so I thought I would share about this "morning papers process" because I always found it so valuable. I have the chance to write freely, every thought, good or bad, nice or not, that I am having. I just did what I wasn't supposed to do… I deleted where I was going with this process. That's why doing this with pen and paper is better than on a computer but I knew I wasn't writing from my heart. Well, I was, in a way. But, with the anger and bitterness at the "powers that shouldn't be" because of the crazy number of forest fires happening right now in Canada and my belief they're not natural and are a part of the "climate change agenda." I cannot see it any other way, knowing what I know about Agenda 2030 and the World Economic Forum, which I have been following for 4 years now. I am so upset that trees, forests, animals, birds, even insects, and our waters, are being used to bring in a way to control human beings, our movement and freedoms even more since covid. My heart breaks and I want to yell from my soapbox that we are being played, manipulated and lied to, again. I cry for nature and I cry that we can't see what is happening because of corrupt media and unelected globalist organizations controlling what we see, hear and thus, perceive. I feel powerless and yet this energizes me too because there is no way I will not take every opportunity to say what I need to say about it to those who will listen and this brings me to what I know is my purpose in life. I can feel it now that I am writing or rather typing this and this macro issues always seems to lead me back to the micro issue of me. I swear to God, I need to trust in myself more and stop censoring myself. Of course, it is hard to believe there is a bogey man called "globalists" out to get us, humanity, but I know it's true and I know I am not alone. Millions of us in the west see it. I am comforted by this.

If I allow myself to go deeply into the heart of this matter for me, this battle between light and dark, our empowerment or our enslavement; my pain for the Earth and nature just being necessary collateral damage in order to to bring about 15-minute cities, digital identification, restrictions on human movement and freedom, is the only reason I want to get up on the rooftop and shout from the rafters for us to wake up. I want to be wrong about the way I see the world now, rather than how I saw it a decade ago. I want to believe in the goodness of government. That's not to say there aren't good people in government, but the institution of government is corrupt, as is medicine, banking, education, military. I have seen this now. The world is upside down and I would do anything to get it right-side up again. I can't "un-see" what I have seen. I took the red-pill. I am glad I did. I wouldn't want this any other way. I just struggle, that is all, to balance being in the world, and not of the world. Being not of the world, means to be free of the man-made systems we live under and have adapted to and adopted as being "life in Earth." They're not, to me. I have had these thoughts for over a year now that I can't rid of. Why, if the Earth gives freely, that we have everything we need available to us for free, why do we have to pay to live? Why do we spend all of our time preparing to earn money ("education") and having to earn money to live on this planet? Is this natural? Does this make any sense, when you dig down into it? Why do we believe we are meant to spend our lives earning money so we can spend our money on having the things we need to live our life? It makes no sense to me when I go into this deep, esoteric, thought process. I feel like I almost leave my body when I go into these ideas. So weird to me and I can't seem to get those around me to see it. I must be nuts even though I know I am not. LOL

I am now 61 and I have never felt that I am walking a tight rope over Niagara Falls like I do now. Balancing the knowing we are being screwed with and the knowing that people don't mean to not know what they don't know. Again, my focus is on the wrong thing here. I need to turn it inward. Who am I going to be? I did write that I want to "be love," so blaming people, getting angry that they don't see it as I do is not love. I just want to cry. My heart breaks for us. I really don't believe we can just look at the positive and be all love and light, without looking at the dark, the negative, and grasp the role it plays in our lives. Why can't I let go of this way of thinking? I dunno. I just think the light can't be used to save us from the dark. You can't use God to avoid pain, frustrations, challenges and difficulties, but to help you through these negative thing. Be a F.R.O.G. "Fully Reliant On God", when need be. But using God to avoid life itself; hoping shit doesn't happen, praying it doesn't happen, is just not the way it works. So the best empowerment is looking into the eyes of the enemy and saying, "No. Not on my watch. You will not get me, my spirit, my heart."

We actually do this all the time when we rise out of the ashes of our personal pain. I just can't help thinking that if we did this on a collective level and really see what's at play in our governments, institutions, and how they have mastered manipulating us, our emotions, how we see and perceive the world, and we all stand up together and say, "No. Not on my watch" would shift life on earth in truly magnificent ways. It's like the wicked witch of the west having boiled water thrown on her, all that nastiness she embodies just melts away. That is the power we hold and the power they are afraid of: our collective voice. If we remain divided through this upcoming time; divided by names and labels, constantly perpetuated by media and governments, and special interest groups, then we will never unite against the true, root cause of chaos in our world. My eyes and my own experience have to be what I ultimately live by. My eyes and my personal experience show me everyday how beautiful human beings really are. I see people of diversity gathering together to enjoy a local rib fest, dancing together to music they love, laughing at comedians who sure know human behaviour and can lovingly mock us. All the loves and likes on a facebook post where one, or several human beings are helping another to safety, or get much needed help financially.

The trucker convoy in Ottawa was a completely different experience than what I later saw on mainstream media. The love flowing through air there was a feeling and sight to behold. Dutch farmers banding together and having their own convoy to stop government takeover of the farmland. People rising up together, not one group against another, but together against a force that continually attempts to divide us. That is beautiful and thrilling to me. That is the reality I love to see. All one in our humanity, celebrating and honouring our diversity, for goodness sake. Live and love all whilst doing no harm. One love. One law.

So that is the end of my morning paper process. I have to confess, it took me sometime to get in to the flow of it. Maybe it will be easy to detect where I eased into the flow of it. Either way, I think this was a fun way to bring my chapter to a close.

Thank you for reading and hearing my voice through these written words.

All the best for a fruitful life that feeds your heart and soul.

Much Love.

Judy

Dedication

I dedicate this chapter to "Life" itself. I don't always like it, but I do always love it. I'm forever grateful.

With my partner, James, in the Black Forest, in Germany. We had our ups and downs at the start of our relationship due to our differing worldviews, but it was worth it to work through them. We have taught each other a lot, and grown together, and individually, in profound ways. We laugh together now more than ever!

I wrote a book," Inner Winner: Finding The Gold That Lies Within". I celebrated with a book launch party in June 2018.

I often felt very empowered in my skates. I had my struggles with skating, both as a skater and coach. But I would not change a thing. I cherish the memories and all the kids I coached, and the coaches I worked with.

Glow up.
Dress well.
Work hard.
Make money.
Educate yourself.

An Infinite Journey

By Anju Malhotra

Life is a tapestry, woven from the unpredictable threads of fate, and my life story seamlessly embodies this notion. I took my first breath in India, arriving as the initial chapter in my young parent's lives. They had settled in a new town, propelled by my father's inaugural government job, with no familiar faces around, where they had to navigate their way independently.

My father, a testament to hard work and kindness, was quick to extend a hand to those in need and to befriend anyone he met. The past few years had exposed him and his family to the harsh realities of financial strain. His father, once a prosperous merchant with a thriving business, had to uproot his family during the partition of the British Indian Empire into India and Pakistan.

The city my grandparents had called home suddenly found itself within the borders of another country, Pakistan, forcing them to leave behind not only their home and business but also the bulk of their possessions. Their transition to Delhi, the newly christened capital of independent India, marked the beginning of a tumultuous chapter.

As the eldest child my father felt the responsibility of assisting his father in providing for the family. He was compelled to seize the first job that came his way, even if it meant departing from his family to work in a distant city.

This commitment was a testament to his character. The narrative unfolded further after his marriage to my mother, as they embarked on the journey of creating a family of their own.

My mother is a remarkable woman, highly educated and very interested in politics. Despite receiving numerous job offers as a school teacher, newspaper columnist, and even a political candidate, she made the selfless choice to become a stay-at-home mom, dedicated to the well-being of her children. Her decision was a testament to her love and devotion.

Her family background was affluent, because of her father's prosperous silk and linen fabric business. However, the turbulence of partition forced her family to leave their business and home behind, seeking refuge in India. They started anew, but fate was cruel, as her father's health faltered, and he departed from this world far too soon. In the wake of his passing, my grandmother, a paragon of grace and courage, took charge of the family's finances, her children, as well as her stepchildren.

The stories my grandmother told of the partition were haunting, filled with the horror of massacres, the poignant memories of parting from friends, heartache of leaving their homes behind with certainty of never returning and the irrevocable changes that affected the migrants.

Resources were scarce for the newly arrived migrants, and this scarcity drew families closer. My childhood memories of my grandparents' home are brimming with images of a bustling house, where love and care filled every corner. Extended family members were frequent visitors, bringing delightful treats, which filled our hearts with joy. Holidays were special because they meant reuniting with cousins. I can still recall the cozy room at the back of the house, where seven of us cousins squeezed onto a double bed, chatting, and giggling for hours. Meanwhile, my grandmother tirelessly prepared lots of food for us as well as the guests who dropped by frequently.

The partition cast a long shadow of fear and insecurity. This anxiety gripped my father, motivating him to work extra hard for job security. He'd put in long hours and often brought work home, embracing the philosophy of frugality and saving for a rainy day. A viewpoint my mother challenged. As a homemaker, she managed the household efficiently, while assisting me with my homework and school activities as well. My father encouraged me to play sports, join NCC and go biking for physical fitness. Whereas my mother nurtured my interests in drama, dance, and music. She was always in the front row, applauding enthusiastically every time I performed on stage.

Many years following Independence passed peacefully. However, when I was a little girl, political unrest between the two countries disrupted our lives. As my family was living in a bordering city, besides the air strikes, the troops deployed war tanks and the danger of civilian attacks loomed. My father, concerned for our safety, urged my mother to leave the city. He urged her to take me and my younger sister to a safer place as soon as possible, but it was not an easy task.

Every day, my father would take us to the railway station with the hope of boarding a train to safety, only to return disappointed. Trains were over-crowded, and people desperately chased after them. My mother, holding my hand and clutching my baby sister, could not secure a spot.

Everyday there was chaos. Frequent radio broadcasts ordered the immediate blackout of lights at night. Sirens blared to warn of possible air strikes, necessitating taking cover and enforcing blackouts after dark. I remember the terror of running to a corner of the room, my tiny hands covering my ears to block the deafening sounds of low-flying fighter planes and bombings. My mother's cooking was often interrupted by shelling, sirens, or air strikes, causing her to trip and spill food. Our lives were far from normal; we ate, slept, and lived in constant fear.

Finally, my father decided to send us with our neighbor who would transport his family and us to a safer town on his tractor trailer in the middle of the night to avoid detection by fighter planes. The family had been trying to catch a train for several days as well without success. Driving at night without turning the headlights on was treacherous due to trenches dug as air raid shelters in every nook and corner of the city and concealed in the darkness. Our neighbor and my father carefully mapped out a road. Reluctantly, my mother packed a small suitcase with essentials and agreed to leave with me and my sister.

I will never forget that night as we rode in an open trailer without any headlights on and on an unfamiliar, seemingly endless road with me clinging to my mother's scarf, gazing at the dark sky with a sense of fear and helplessness. None of us knew if we would reach our destination safely. The thunderous roars of fighter planes and fiery air strikes periodically punctuated the darkness. Each time I would close my eyes and hold my mother even tighter, listening to her whispered prayers.

We drove through the night, my heart racing, until at dawn we were welcomed by many kind-hearted individuals who offered us food, water, and hot tea. Tears streamed down my mother's cheeks as we disembarked from the trailer. We had arrived in the historical city of Jaito, somewhat shielded from land troops. But my thoughts were consumed with worry for my father, who had to remain behind because of his job. I was grateful for our safety but deeply concerned about him.

We were taken to a building resembling a motel, where several families had found refuge. War has a way of bringing out the worst in people, turning the reasonable into the irrational, the fair into the unfair. Yet, where we were staying, I witnessed the opposite. People shared their food, clothes, and even money with each other. They laughed and cried together, proving that in the face of adversity, at humanity's core remains love and compassion. This experience, at a young age, instilled in me a profound love for humanity and the understanding that love is far more potent than hatred. Although I was too young to realize how this had affected me, it led me to embark on various humanitarian projects later in my life. We stayed at the city of Jaito for over a month and finally reunited with my father after the ceasefire.

From an early age, my aunt and uncle, who were my mom's sister and brother-in-law, embraced me as their own, treating me with the same love and care as they would their own daughter. I often moved between these two families, experiencing the joy of being cherished by both. My aunt resided in Mumbai, a bustling cosmopolitan city celebrated for its open-mindedness and diverse cultures. In contrast, my parents lived in a smaller city characterized by more traditional values and ways of life.

While growing up my consciousness had always been attuned to social issues, and the glaring inequality in gender roles and expectations was something that deeply concerned me. Though at home, I did not feel any different, I observed the stark contrast in the way society celebrated the birth of a son as opposed to a daughter. The birth of a son was often met with exuberant enthusiasm, while a daughter's arrival was often treated with less importance, particularly if there were already other daughters in the family. I noticed this societal pattern more prominently in my parent's city than my aunts place of residence, Mumbai.

This disparity may have been in part a consequence of the dowry system prevalent in India, although it is thankfully waning in influence today. Under this system, a girl's parents were obligated to provide a substantial dowry to the groom and his family during their daughter's wedding. The sheer concept of this system was a staggering blow to a girl's self-esteem, as it insinuated that her worth was determined by the amount of money and possessions she could bring into the marriage. It is no surprise that in less affluent families, the birth of a girl was often met with mixed emotions.

The situation was exacerbated by the societal expectation that once married, the bride's parents were to adopt a passive, non-interfering stance in her life, despite having provided a substantial dowry. Conversely, the newlywed bride was expected to seamlessly assimilate into her husband's family dynamics without expressing any grievances. She was supposed to prioritize her husband's family's customs and preferences over her own needs and familial obligations, effectively transforming herself into an unrealistic "Devi" (goddess) possessing superhero-like abilities to gracefully manage every aspect of her new life.

While numerous women rejected these conditions, many young women tended to go along to maintain the social image of good bahus (daughter in laws). In the pursuit of being liked and accepted by everyone, she often sacrificed her self-worth. Bollywood films also depicted these women as idols, setting them up as exemplars for society to follow.

I could not stand idly by in the face of this injustice. I actively protested against the dowry system using my voice and writing articles in the newspapers to encourage girls and their parents to break free from this oppressive tradition. Many of my friends did that as well. Unfortunately, the system was so deeply entrenched that people resorted to various tactics to extract a dowry. Some employed indirect methods, sending relatives to ask for it under different guises, such as presenting gifts or offering assistance to the newlyweds while others made outright demands just before the wedding. The only way out of this was the financial independence of women. I decided to pursue the highest level of education and achieve financial independence which is what most women at present have done in India and many other countries.

My dreams of becoming a doctor were a defining part of my journey. While in university, I took the entrance exam to get admission in the medical school but unfortunately my initial attempt fell short. Determined not to be deterred, I made up my mind to try again after another year. However, fate had other plans in store for me. It was during this time that my grandmother extended an invitation for us to visit her in Delhi city. Little did I know that this trip would change the course of my life.

In Delhi, I was introduced to the man who would later become my husband. The idea of considering marriage was not something I had anticipated. My grandmother was familiar with his family background, and when his family approached her, she thought he was a great match for me. She convinced everyone in our family and finally I agreed to go out with him for a couple of weeks to get to know him before making and decision.

The concept of arranged marriages may sound unconventional to some, but in India, it had often proven to be a successful practice. Families looked beyond the initial love connection between two people, carefully considering other factors that contribute to the longevity of the marital institution. Though I preferred meeting someone on my own I was not opposed to the idea. I wanted to get to know him before deciding though and once that was done and we both agreed the wedding was arranged within a remarkably short span of ten days.

Soon after, I found myself on a airplane to Canada, beginning a new chapter of my life at a very young age. I was leaving behind the familiarity of my homeland and embarking on a journey to a foreign country to be with my husband whom I had only met a few weeks ago. The experience was a mix of excitement for a fresh start and the fear of an unknown life in an unfamiliar place.

In my earlier years, I had been exceptionally social, forming deep connections with numerous friends both in school, college, and my neighborhood. Being the first child in both my maternal and paternal families, I had developed particularly close bonds with my younger sibling and cousins as well.

Upon landing in Canada, I was faced with the challenge of limited communication with my parents and other family members. The expense of international calls back then meant our conversations were often brief, lasting no more than a minute or two. Though I was trying to settle down in Canada I was constantly missing my family, friends and the hustle and bustle of my busy hometown. The distance from my loved ones was a poignant reminder of the significant changes I had undertaken in my life. Many times, I regretted my decision to come to Canada.

At first, I found solace in staying indoors, trying to keep myself occupied. However, as the days passed, a profound sense of loneliness enveloped me, particularly when my husband left for work. Homesickness intensified, frequently bringing tears to my eyes. It became evident that I needed to break free from this isolation, establish connections, build friendships, and Integrate myself into the Canadian way of life."

My arrival in Canada also marked the beginning of a journey where I had to acquire a multitude of new skills. I was essentially starting from scratch, I did not know how to cook, do housework and comprehending the Canadian accent presented its own set of challenges. The unfamiliar transit system added to my sense of disorientation, and arriving in the heart of a harsh winter made even stepping outside a daunting task.

It's important to note that this was a time when google, social media, laptops and cell phones were not available. Exploration was a far more challenging endeavour back then. With resolve, I started with simple steps. I began walking to the nearby grocery store and other local shops every day, initiating conversations with people along the way. My first significant connection in Canada came when I met an Indian woman at the grocery store. She was working and encouraged me to seek employment as well. Thanks to her, I secured my first job in Canada at her place of employment. I only worked there for a few months though as I wanted to go back to the university

My plan to return to the university was disrupted after having my Indian education credentials assessed, unexpectedly resulting in a setback of two years. I also discovered I was pregnant a week before getting this news, realizing that my academic journey would be prolonged. I decided to explore other options and enrolled in a computer programming course at a community college. The college was located far from our place of residence, leading us to relocate closer to it before the course began. Thankfully, a friend of my husband, residing nearby, generously offered us a room for rent in his house which we gratefully accepted.

As my course commenced, we settled into a decently sized room in a five-bedroom house. Despite the house having a spacious kitchen, we encountered an issue. One of the homeowners preferred exclusive access to the kitchen at her preferred times, which made it difficult for me to cook according to my schedule. Since I was pregnant, and my cooking hours were very limited I often ended up eating at the college canteen. I was vegetarian and hated the smell of cheese during pregnancy, so I lived on baked potatoes, french fries and bagels for most of the time.

Upon the completion of my course, we moved to a rented apartment. Shortly after my graduation, we joyfully welcomed our first child into the world. When my daughter was a few months old, I embarked on the pursuit of employment. Subsequently, I secured a job and arranged for childcare by engaging a babysitter within our residential complex. As a young mother, entrusting my infant to the care of a babysitter throughout the day was a challenging decision, yet it seemed the most viable option at that time. Unfortunately, within a few days, I observed worrisome changes in my baby's behavior. She exhibited signs of lethargy, excessive sleepiness, and a departure from her usual vibrant and active behaviour at home.

Concerned about her well-being, I promptly scheduled a visit to the pediatrician for a thorough evaluation. During the examination it revealed that she appeared in good health and spirits during the weekends but exhibited distressing behavior on weekdays. Additionally, reports from other parents surfaced, indicating concerns about the quality of care provided by the babysitter. It became evident that there were discrepancies in the care provided. In light of these concerns, I made the difficult decision to resign from my job and stay at home with my daughter until she turned one year old.

When my daughter reached the age of one and began attending daycare, I resumed my job search. I managed to secure employment twice, although neither position aligned with my qualifications and lasted no more than a few months. It was a frustrating period of job instability. However, with the assistance of a manpower agency, I eventually secured a position in a sizable company.

At this new workplace, my manager, originally from Mumbai, India, proved to be an exceptional boss. Alongside, my supervisor, a warm-hearted person with a fantastic sense of humor, provided consistent support. Regrettably, it was during this job that I encountered discrimination for the first time. Despite facing unfair treatment from my co-workers, I refrained from disclosing this to anyone due to the fear of jeopardizing my job security.

Around the same time, some family members had immigrated to Canada and were living with us. While their presence was undoubtedly helpful in many ways, it also introduced its own share of stresses. The new responsibilities at home added to the already complex dynamic and balancing these with workplace issues proved to be challenging.

The mounting pressure at work eventually became too much to bear, compelling me to discuss workplace discrimination with my manager. He astutely recognized the issue and promptly called a meeting. In this gathering, he warned my co-workers of the potential consequences. This intervention did lead to some improvements in the workplace environment, although the transformation was far from complete.

Dealing with discrimination is a profoundly trying experience. It chips away at one's self-esteem, leaving a sense of degradation and belittlement. Throughout this challenging period, I found immense support from my supervisor, who consistently encouraged me to stand up for myself. Individuals like him contribute to making the world a better place to live. With time, the situation did ameliorate, and I formed friendships with some of my colleagues. I persevered in that role for under four years, proving that resilience and a supportive environment can ultimately triumph over adversity.

We moved into a new home when I became pregnant with my second daughter. I decided to take a leave of absence to care for my new baby. After a year or so, I embarked on a job search once more and landed a position in a much larger company. This opportunity held the promise of better career growth. I was one of the three women in the department, as the IT field remained largely dominated by men.

The work environment was more favorable than my previous job, but there was a recurrent issue that could not be ignored for too long. Whenever a new and promising job opening emerged, it was invariably filled by a male candidate. The most significant blow came after a few years when a male coworker, whom I had personally trained was hired for a new position for which I had also applied.

I decided to confront my manager about this seemingly unfair decision. To my surprise, he nonchalantly dismissed my concerns, explaining that, while I was undoubtedly more qualified, I was not the right candidate for the job. His reasoning was that I probably wouldn't be available for overtime on the weekends due to my family responsibilities as a woman with young children. What troubled me most was that he had not even taken the time to ask me if I would be available or not.

It was a stark moment of realization. I felt discriminated once again, this time not because of my color but for being a woman and a mother. I couldn't comprehend why women were being treated this way. This contrasted sharply with my upbringing back home, where my parents had never made me feel inferior to my male counterparts. In fact, I was proudly held up as a role model by my aunts and uncles for their children. I had certainly encountered societal gender biases in my homeland, but I had assumed Canada with its reputation for being more advanced and progressive would be different. Yet here I was, feeling disrespected and humiliated on account of my gender and maternal role.

After this incident the work environment had become increasingly burdensome, making each day feel like a struggle. I knew that I could not continue working there for too long. My yearly vacation was coming due, so I decided to visit my parents and take time to reflect on the path ahead. Tragically, upon my return our lives took an unexpected turn on the way back from a routine shopping trip. A severe car accident shook our world when another vehicle skidded into our car head-on on the highway. Both my husband and I sustained injuries, but I bore the brunt of the impact. The accident left me with significant back and shoulder pain, making restful nights a distant memory.

The ordeal took a toll not only on me physically but mentally as well. My path to recovery involved an extensive regimen of physiotherapy and later psychotherapy as well. Initially, I was hesitant believing that people consulted psychotherapists only when they were severely mentally unwell. However, my doctor assured me that this was not the case and that I could discontinue anytime. As I embarked on the journey of psychotherapy, I realized its benefits. It provided me with a platform to vocalize my frustrations and provided tools to deal with the same.

As I gradually recovered from the car accident, I began contemplating a significant career change. A while back, a sales manager from the computer sales department crossed paths with me in the office cafeteria. During our conversation, he suggested that I consider a career in computer sales, assuring me that my personality and communication skills were well-suited for the role. He even extended a job offer, featuring a basic salary along with commissions. The idea intrigued me, but I had never dabbled in sales, and doubts loomed large. How could I persuade others to buy from me? What if I faltered in this new endeavor? Regrettably, I had declined the offer.

However, the idea of a sales career refused to fade away. It beckoned to me as an avenue that could lead to becoming my own boss. I revisited the thought and engaged with the sales manager once again. A sales position had opened up, but it entailed frequent travel outside the city, something I was reluctant to undertake. As I contemplated the prospects of a career in sales, the appeal of being in charge of my destiny grew stronger with each passing day.

My husband, who had established a successful career in sales with an insurance company, had steadily climbed the ranks and earned a promotion to a management position. He proposed that I explore a sales career within his company. Since I had not committed to the sales position in computer sales, I decided to explore this opportunity.

After a successful job interview, I immediately began the process of obtaining the necessary licenses, eventually embarking on my first sales job. My training of two weeks proved invaluable in preparing me for the role. I was assigned to a different branch office, distinct from my husband's.

I approached my new role with unwavering focus, diligence, and a go-getter attitude. Each week, I dialed hundreds of numbers, undeterred by the initial rejections I encountered. To bolster my spirits, I placed a prominent smiley face on my desk, and every time someone hung up on me or declined, I would glance at the smiley face, put on a smile, and make the next call. My belief in the value of the insurance products I was selling was unwavering.

As time passed, I honed my skills, growing more confident and proficient at effectively communicating my message over the phone. I transitioned from making calls to securing numerous appointments with potential clients, which eventually translated into successful sales. The more I achieved, the harder I worked, and the rewards followed. Moreover, I noticed that I was feeling a profound sense of job satisfaction as I was helping people protect their family's future and making a difference.

I reached a milestone when I qualified for the prestigious leaders' conference. To mark this achievement, I decided to pay a visit to my former employer. Walking into my former manager's office, I thanked him for not promoting me earlier. I had discovered a newfound self-assurance and was no longer concerned with past grievances. The encounter left me with a sense of closure.

Yet, my ambitions soared higher, as I aspired to qualify for another conference. While I had ambitious career goals, my guiding principle remained firmly rooted in putting the client's needs first, not my own financial gain. My work was a source of pride, it involved securing families' financial well-being and offering them peace of mind. I continued to excel in the industry until an opportunity arose that would take my career in a new direction.

I had met a manager of a real estate office who encouraged me to consider a transition to real estate. He assured me that I had the potential to excel even further, enjoying greater flexibility and opportunities for success. I had long held a fascination for various types of homes, pouring over home and garden magazines and even driving through neighborhoods to admire houses. Having already tasted success in selling intangible products, I was now eager to delve into the world of real estate where I could market something tangible, something people could touch, feel, and see. The real estate market was thriving, so I wasted no time in pursuing the necessary licenses.

Within a few months, I found myself working in a real estate office, set in a brand-new building. The office was not only aesthetically pleasing but also housed a team of high-achieving professionals and an exceptional support staff. The stark contrast from my previous career was that I had no leads to rely on, I was starting from scratch.

My familiarity with cold calling proved to be an asset, but I soon discovered another tool in the real estate trade: door knocking. We often worked in a team, which made the initially awkward task of approaching stranger's homes more bearable. While some people chose not to answer the door or responded brusquely, most were amicable when met face to face. I gradually built a database of potential clients. I completed a few successful home sales and reinvested the proceeds in advertising. I took to promoting my services in the local newspaper, on the radio, and in real estate magazines. This was a time before Google and portable cell phones were still relatively rare.

Although people saw my ads, they often found it challenging to recall my name, prompting me to incorporate a distinctive approach. I printed a picture of the Taj Mahal on my business card, accompanied by a tagline: "If the Taj Mahal were for sale, I would get it sold." My consistent newspaper advertising reinforced my association with this iconic image. When people could not remember my name, they would call my office and ask for someone with Taj Mahal on her ads. As my business started picking up, I knew I had made the right career move.

Through my business was thriving my personal life was experiencing turbulence. The traditional thinking that, as a woman, my primary responsibility should be managing the household, not pursuing a career weighed heavily on me. Despite consistently achieving the sales awards, I felt dissatisfied and unhappy. In spite of my efforts, I could not make it all work. I was under a lot of stress which had started to affect my health.

Some time later I was invited to a party at a friend's house. There was singing and dancing and everyone was enjoying themselves. While there suddenly I noticed some unusual swelling and redness in the joints of my hands. I also started to experience peculiar, uncomfortable sensations in my fingers and wrists. By late evening, the pain had intensified to such a degree that I had to leave. I sat in my car to drive but could not even turn the steering wheel to back my car out of the driveway. I assumed it was some sort of virus, especially since I also felt slightly feverish.

Upon arriving home, I went to bed thinking that the discomfort would subside by the morning. To my dismay, the pain only intensified with each passing day. Concerned, I sought medical attention, undergoing a battery of tests that ultimately led to a diagnosis: Rheumatoid arthritis. I was taken aback with the diagnosis as arthritis was commonly associated with older individuals and I was and I was young.

My doctor referred me to a rheumatologist, who shed light on the nature of my condition. He explained that I had an autoimmune disease, in which my immune cells had mistakenly attacked my own joint cells. He emphasized that age had no bearing on the onset of this ailment. I was prescribed medication and provided with referrals for various therapies. The pain was most acute in the mornings, and while the medication helped during the day, the discomfort would invariably return at night. This prompted regular visits for physiotherapy and hot wax treatments several times a week.

Over time, the condition worsened, affecting my wrists, knees, toes, and fingers. To manage the pain, I had to resort to wearing wrist braces that limited joint movement and special shoes. On one occasion, when my husband accompanied me to a nearby mall, I realized with great dismay that I could not walk even a few yards to reach the store I wanted to go to. I had to sit on a bench, waiting for my husband to get a wheelchair.

As I observed older individuals navigating the mall on their feet, I had a newfound appreciation for the simple act of walking, something I had once taken for granted.

Despite my youth I found myself unable to walk even a short distance. A few weeks later my stomach began to experience unusual spasms accompanied by pain. This distressing development made eating difficult, leading to significant weight loss. Over the course of seven months, my wrist joint had become fused, some finger joints had changed shape, and I lived with persistent stomach discomfort.

During a visit to my doctor, I was introduced a brand-new medication to manage my condition. As a prudent measure, I thoroughly examined the medication's fine print and became deeply concerned. There was a small risk associated with this drug potentially affecting my vision and even leading to blindness. Understandably I was consumed by anxiety and reluctance to use this medication.

A friend came to visit and wholeheartedly recommended alternative medicine and treatments. He spoke to me about a Naturopathy center in Bangalore, India.

Intrigued, I decided to look into it. I reached out to the center, providing details of my medical history in an application. In just a few days, I received a response indicating that for any meaningful results, I would need to commit to a stay at the center for at least 40 days. Since I was in so much pain I decided to embark on this journey and booked my treatment immediately.

Considering that I had young children at the time who needed to be taken care of, my husband graciously agreed to do so with the help of his parents. I packed my bags and boarded a plane to India within a few days. The flight attendants provided excellent assistance throughout the journey to make me comfortable.

Upon landing in Bangalore India, a car was ready to take me to the Naturopathy center. I was greeted with a warm welcome upon arrival at the center and was taken to a cozy hut surrounded by lush greenery, imbuing the entire environment with a sense of tranquility. I settled into my new surroundings, and the very next day, after consultations with different doctors, my treatment was planned. I was prescribed a three-week liquid fast and several natural therapies and physiotherapy sessions.

The first week proved particularly challenging, as it was accompanied by a flood of negative emotions and sadness. However, this emotional turbulence gradually improved. My daily schedule was packed with treatments during the day, but in the evening I found time for socializing and reading. Some nights featured cooking classes and lectures by the doctors as well.

During my stay, I absorbed a wealth of knowledge, delving into topics such as the profound impact of food on our health, the relationship between stress and illness and techniques for managing it. Consequently, I became well-versed in yoga, pranayama, and meditation. Every night, I diligently documented my newfound knowledge which included healthy food ideas and recipes, yoga asanas, exercise routines, pranayama techniques, meditation techniques for stress management and home remedies.

Upon my return home, I immediately implemented significant lifestyle changes. While my pain had considerably improved during my stay at the naturopathy center, I had not yet fully recovered and I was to follow the diet and at home treatments. Upon rejoining the workforce, I made a concerted effort to allocate more time to self-care. I brought homemade meals to work and adhered to a strict dietary regimen. I was also to go back every six months to the center for further treatment and I did. After a few years I had fully recovered.

Few years later I wanted to have another child and with the grace of God I became pregnant with my third child. The first three months of the pregnancy proceeded as expected, similar to my previous ones. However, starting in the fourth month, I began experiencing a great deal of pain. An ultrasound revealed that I had developed fibroids, and as the baby grew, these fibroids also increased in size, leading to severe discomfort. I found myself in the emergency room on multiple occasions due to excruciating pain.

The situation became dire to the extent that some doctors recommended considering an abortion. However, I could not bring myself to accept this suggestion. Instead, I consulted my family doctor, who reassured me and referred me to a high-risk pregnancy gynecologist in Toronto. Under their care and treatment, I was fortunate enough to have a healthy baby boy.

Slowly life became normal. I was enjoying motherhood again and after a few months resumed work with a balanced approach. My parents had immigrated to Canada along with my younger sister and that was a very happy time for me. I had missed them for so many years. The unconditional love and care was so heartwarming. The good times did not last too long though. After staying and working here for a few years my father went back home with my mom for a visit but decided not to comeback.

Few years passed and I encountered another significant health challenge which required surgery. While recuperating from a surgical procedure, my family and I embarked on a brief ski trip. Although my intention was to relax at the hotel while my husband and son enjoyed skiing over a long weekend, our return journey was marred by a severe car accident. Our vehicle skidded off a cliff due to black ice, plunging fifty feet and rolling twice before settling sideways in a ditch. The impact threw our ski gear out of the car, my son into the pathfinder's trunk, and resulted in injuries to my husband's forehead, as well as severe harm to my right arm, back, and legs. Fortunately, passersby called emergency services and rendered aid despite the leaking gas from our vehicle. Someone assisted my son while I urgently called out my husband's name. The police remarked that it was a nearly fatal accident, expressing disbelief at our survival.

I had encountered moments near death, watching my car soar through the air among the treetops and plummet into a ditch. In those harrowing moments, as the car rolled, my instinct was to somehow shield my son, and upon landing, my frantic search for him in the back seat was the most terrifying moments.

Despite enduring substantial pain, I came to understand that it wasn't my time to depart this world yet. I realized that I had a bigger purpose. As I could not return to my regular work, I began investing time in my passion for music, something I was not finding time to do much being busy with the family and work. I used to perform in a band and on TV some years back but later I could not. Engaging in music again became a significant factor in my healing process, providing moments of respite from my physical pain.

I had been introduced to the Art of Living foundation many years ago where I had learned Sudershan Kriya, a unique breathwork technique which I had been practicing off and on, but this was the time for integrating yoga and breath work into my daily routine once again. This regimen notably enhanced both my physical and mental well-being. Furthermore, delving deeper into spirituality, I commenced volunteering at the Art of Living foundation, discovering immense joy in contributing to the betterment of humanity. This experience marked the beginning of my journey toward aiding and supporting others in need.

I initiated a project which became my annual endeavor, providing non-perishable groceries to needy families, essential medicines to senior homes, and educational support to underprivileged children back home. I now believe that the universe operates on a simple principle: when you dedicate your energy to giving, you receive effortlessly in return.

The recovery from the physical and emotional toll of that incident as well as illness took more than three years. It reshaped my perception of life profoundly. I came to cherish each day, realizing that tomorrow is never guaranteed. This awareness prompted me to keep engaging in humanitarian causes, contributing my time to initiatives aimed at making a positive impact in the world along with resuming my real estate profession which I love.

My humanitarian efforts garnered recognition through several accolades, such as the "Woman of Substance," "One of 50 Most Influential Women," "Woman Hero," "Global Icon of Women," and a "Certificate of Commitment" in the Guinness Book of World Records UK to name a few. Despite these honors, I remain steadfast in feeling there is always more to be done. I strongly believe that our profession or passion can be channeled for the betterment of society. When work is carried out with such intent, the outcomes are profound.

I reignited my musical pursuits, recording a single and re-entering the professional music sphere. I firmly believe in spreading joy through the art of music. I love to perform at different events, fundraisers and stage shows to do the same. I had also written, composed, and performed a song for a Canadian film. Most of the money received from singing performances has been donated for the education of the underprivileged children one at a time. My dream is to educate many more.

I ventured into TV show hosting alongside my passion for music. One of my shows was titled "Jee Le Zindgi," translating to "Live Life to the Fullest." The aim of this show was to inspire the audiences to embrace and cherish life by watching various talented guests and their stories. Regrettably, the studio ceased operations due to the challenges posed by the Covid pandemic. I also hosted a health-focused talk show featuring various doctors and healthcare experts.

Amid the challenges of the Covid era, I initiated the project called "Talk to Me," offering a non-judgmental platform for individuals battling sadness and loneliness. Unexpectedly, the initiative became a source of purpose for me. Each day, I eagerly prepared to connect with people via zoom, phone calls and in person. This kept me very busy throughout Covid times.

They say where there is a will there is a way. During Covid period I also got an opportunity to enroll in an online filmmaking course. Having co-produced a film a few years back, this was a chance to expand my skills. After the course ended, my team and I embarked on the journey of making a short film. The story was inspired by the real-life story of two American teenagers, shedding light on mental health challenges faced by young adults. The film is called "The Backpack" which I co-directed and also did the art direction for it.

In 2023 I received funding to make another film in collaboration with other filmmakers titled "Food for Thought," which is based on the topic of food insecurity. The film is aimed to change the public perception of the individuals who access food banks. This film has screened at six film festivals so far and received Best Shorts award at Toronto International Nollywood Film Festival and Audience choice award at the Indigo Moon Festival.

After the two films I also wrote, directed, and produced a theatrical play called "The Untold Story," which was inspired by the real-life experiences of one woman which really mirrored many others. It resonated with the audience, selling out four consecutive shows at a local theater. By assembling a diverse cast for the play, my aim was to convey through storytelling that emotions transcend color, affecting everyone universally.

I reignited my childhood passion for acting as well and landed a role in a TV commercial which had marked the commencement of my acting career. Later it led to roles in short films, more brand commercials, and a Canadian television series "The Potluck Ladies" which is to be aired in 2024. And this is my first effort to write a summarized story of some of my life's journey. It surely has been an emotional and awakening experience.

I firmly believe that life is an ever-evolving journey, often veering off the planned path. Embracing the flow of each moment, whether good or bad, is the key. Nothing remains permanent, and enduring permanence might eventually breed monotony. My son once imparted a valuable lesson: life comprises a collection of experiences, and by making each one memorable, life becomes interesting and joyful. I strive to live by this ethos daily, aiming to derive value from each experience and make a positive difference, no matter how small in someone's life.

And the life journey continues…

Dedication

An infinite journey is a heartfelt tribute to the unwavering courage, resilience, and determination that have been the cornerstone of my life's journey. It is dedicated to the extraordinary individuals whose constant support, love, and guidance have enriched my narrative and shaped my path.

To my beloved mother, the bedrock of my existence and the guiding light that illuminated my earliest days. Her boundless love and endless sacrifices built the foundation upon which I stand today. From the earliest stage performances to the fancy dress competitions that fueled my confidence, her steady presence and support were unwavering. Her spiritual guidance nurtured my soul and her firm belief in my abilities constantly reminded me of my worth and potential. Her tears shed for me during moments of joy and struggle were testament to her deep empathy and love.

To my father, whose quiet strength and unspoken guidance shaped my understanding of resilience and perseverance. At an early age, his insistence that I learn music from a professional teacher he hired for me was not appreciated by me, but I am so grateful to him now. His kindness towards the less fortunate was a recurring lesson that deeply impacted me, inspiring me to embark on the path of humanitarian work.

To Oprah Winfrey, whose show I watched on TV almost daily and whose words of wisdom and relentless pursuit of positivity became a guiding force during my darkest moments, inspiring me to keep moving forward.

To my cherished friend Sangeeta Arora, whose consistent presence and empathetic ear provided comfort and strength during moments of uncertainty and despair.

To Mamta Katarey, whose guidance and support when needed, both personally and professionally, have been a steady anchor in navigating life's tumultuous waters.

To Rama, a dear friend from 9th grade whose enduring friendship, transcending geographical boundaries and time, has been a source of comforting childhood playfulness and boundless love.

To my sister Anita Dabra, a great soul whose kindness, spiritual wisdom, and unconditional support have been a consistent source of guidance and comfort, demonstrating her unending love and loyalty.

Finally, to my whole family for standing by me.

With immeasurable gratitude and boundless love,

Anju Malhotra

The Untold Story

Biography

Introducing Suzy Tamasy, a trailblazing CEO, Publisher, and Creator making waves in the entrepreneurial and finance realms with her innovative ventures. As the visionary behind SuzyQJewels, Frugal Divas, Empowered in Heels, Biz & Fashion Magazine, and Women on Biz, Suzy's journey began with a passion for fashion and an unwavering work ethic. From her roots as a jewelry designer using recycled materials, she has evolved into a dynamic entrepreneur, now leading a virtual consignment shop and a cutting-edge clothing line.

What sets Suzy apart is not just her business acumen but her profound commitment to social impact. Within her SuzyQJewels and Frugal Divas clothing lines, a percentage of sales goes towards supporting women's shelters in Ontario. Suzy, a prolific blogger, event producer, and serial entrepreneur, is not merely a talker but a doer. Each year, she organizes a Swap, Sell, and Donate event along with a fashion show, where her symbolic walk represents breaking the cycle of abuse and standing against violence.

Suzy's philosophy revolves around fostering connections and inspiring her clients to pursue their dreams relentlessly. Based in Oshawa, Ontario, and a mother of two sons, Suzy Tamasy is more than a name – she embodies beauty, intelligence, and business savvy. Explore the world of SuzyQJewels to witness the seamless convergence of style, intellect, and entrepreneurial spirit that defines Suzy Tamasy's remarkable journey. Currently pursuing her Ph.D. in psychology, Suzy aims to continue her mission of assisting women and children in breaking the cycle of abuse. Award winner of 2024 of the Canadian Choice Awards for digital marketing/advertising for BizFashion.

Aceso is a counselor and entrepreneur living in downtown Toronto. She studied Science and Psychology and is seeking to complete her Masters in Psychotherapy. Her passion and dream is to help people improve mental well-being.

Anju Malhotra is a multifaceted individual excelling as a Singer, Actor, Filmmaker, TV Host, Realtor, and above all, a committed Humanitarian. Her overarching mission is to incite change by using various media platforms such as films, theatre, and television to raise awareness about societal issues and causes.

As the host of the show "Jee Lee Zindgi" on South Asian TV, Anju inspired viewers to embrace life to the fullest by interviewing change makers across various domains such as visual arts, music, literature, leadership, healthcare, and entrepreneurship. Additionally, she engaged with audiences live on another show, addressing crucial social issues and life skills.

Anju's acting portfolio includes commercials, short films, and an upcoming Canadian TV series titled "The Potluck Ladies," set for release in 2024. She notably wrote, directed, and produced the play "The Untold Story," based on a woman's life, garnering immense appreciation across four full house shows.

With her extensive work in the film industry, Anju produced and directed two short films and a feature film, all adeptly addressing pertinent social concerns through compelling storytelling. Her feature film received recognition at the IFFSA Canada and various international film festivals. "The Backpack," a short film, earned praise during its screening at Cineplex Mississauga. Her latest short film, "Food for Thought," secured selections in six film festivals, earning both the Best Short and Audience Choice awards.

Anju has showcased her vocal prowess at numerous stage shows, participating in fundraisers, festivals, and private events. Her contribution as a vocalist in the Canadian Musical Documentary Film "Kadupul" is noteworthy. Through her music, she actively supports initiatives providing free education to underprivileged children in rural areas and contributes to the "Give a Gift of Smile" project, supplying non-perishable food to the needy during Christmas in India.

Recognized as a community leader, social worker, and advocate for volunteerism, Anju has served on several nonprofit boards and organized numerous fundraising events, including the Trillium Diwali Gala and Lions Club Gala. She played an integral role in managing events for the Art of Living Foundation and spearheaded the GTA's significant International Yoga Day event for three consecutive years. Her leadership extended to women's associations, organizing workshops and projects for women's empowerment, and initiatives for mental wellness among seniors and cancer patients through the "Soothe and Groove" project of the Cancer Warrior Foundation.

Her professional achievements in the financial and real estate sectors have earned Anju Malhotra several Top Achievement Awards, alongside numerous accolades for her humanitarian endeavours. She has been honoured with titles such as Woman of Substance, Woman Hero, "50 Most Influential Women," Walk of Fame Winner, and International Icon of Women 2022. Anju was recognized by Biz and Fashion magazine as one of the Top 50 women to watch in 2021 and received the World Book of Record London Certificate of Commitment for her global humanitarian efforts during the Covid-19 pandemic.

Judy Swallow is a former competitive figure skater and coached skating for 40 years. While at a training camp in Lake Placid, NY when she was 15, she had her first real introduction to the mental aspect of sport in a workshop, that struck a chord within her and really sparked her love for psychology which soon became her passion.

As she began to pay closer attention to her inner feelings of inadequacy and the lack of belief in herself, this drove her to study and delve deeply into the subject of Psychology, Consciousness and Mindfulness and has been doing so since her 20's.

This choice leads her step by step to cultivate a practice of self-awareness that enabled her to understand and undo the beliefs and programming that she held within, which has taken her from feeling insecure, to now claiming her presence in the world, and finding her authentic voice and expression.

Judy Gaw is a retired Entrepreneur and living in Gananoque, Ontario. Judy has a second-degree level Reiki Healer, an eCPR Practitioner, and a graduate of the Stephen Ministry.

Judys entrepreneurial spirit is still alive thru being a Super Patch Partner and a Pampered Chef host.

Judy lives with her husband Hugh and works on continuing to heal both physically and mentally from her stroke.

Amina Bhanji lived in Africa as a young child during a political crisis. She was raised by her eldest brother and sister-in-law. She emigrated to England then to Canada in 1975. Her family went through the many challenges as new immigrants in the "land of opportunity." By following her passions, she found her purpose. Today, she is a Human Resources professional, certified Trainer and Coach, a Distinguished Toastmaster and a Professional Development Advisor for the Ontario Public Service. She is also the founder of Kindness Through Self Care. In her spare time, she loves to volunteer, and fund raise for worthy causes close to her heart. She is the mother of two amazing daughters. Amina can be located in Toronto.

I am a single Mom to 4 kiddos. They have taught me so much as a mother, daughter, woman and business woman. I was born and raised on my family farm in Bengough Saskatchewan. My childhood was not easy. I was bullied in school by peers and teachers. I was never into sports; it wasn't my thing to have to be on the school volleyball or basketball team. I was involved in figure skating, curling and karate. Karate was my passion. Karate was where I had my first taste of what I wanted and what made my heart beat faster. I learnt so much during my 10 years of karate. I achieved my 2nd degree brown belt; I earned a spot on team Saskatchewan to go to Canadians and I earned the title of COMMA (Canadian Open Martial Arts Association) Champion. I would take lessons up to 3 times a week and weekends were dedicated to tournaments. Mom and I travelled everywhere. She was my biggest fan. Through karate I was introduced to Reiki.

My passion. I am a double Reiki Master I achieved during COVID and now have a small Reiki business. Reiki has taught me so much about myself. I have met so many amazing souls that each and everyone of them has touched and held space for me. Everything happens for a reason and one journey leads you to another journey. Our destiny is ours and we can create our own destiny. All we have to do is believe in the magic of ourselves.

Helping our Community get noticed!

Meet Xanthi Theo with her words!

SEEK THE TREASURE TROVE

By: Xanthi Theo

All of us are shooting stars

All of us are expensive cars

To be silenced is preposterous

Individuality is gold

It's not pretentious, you mustn't question

We make a mistake just to learn a lesson

Some days can be hideous

Repeating our mistakes is insidious

Master acceptance

And now you found rubies and sapphires

I wrote this poem for those who feel they aren't heard, are repressed and have low self-esteem. I wrote it for those who let fear get in the way of achieving accomplishments. I wrote it for those who missed opportunities because they were shy. I wrote it for those who feel small. Each one of us is rare or unique and all of us are gifts from God. We all make a difference in life whether it's simply making somebody happy or supporting your local business or being a front-line worker. When we follow the herd, we lose our identity and it leaves no room for self-expression, personality, thoughts and opinions. Furthermore, accepting our mistakes is important. Learning to accept is a stepping stone to stop repeating our mistakes over and over again.

To order a copy of 'Your Twinkle's Impact - A Collection of Inspirational Poetry and Art Please contact Xanthi Theo on instagram:

IG: @xt3blue T-shirts of her poetry are also available in any size.

YOUR TWINKLE'S IMPACT – A COLLECTION OF INSPIRATIONAL POETRY AND ART

By: Xanthi Theo

My name is Xanthi Theo. I grew up in Toronto, one of the best cities in the world. I like to inspire others because I see the good in people. I like going on nature walks because they clear my head and help me think. I like to visit museums because they are part of art which is all around us and part of our heritage and who we are. In fact, I worked at a museum which I enjoyed doing because I was part of October Fest which involved the selling of homemade jams and garden activities such as croquet. I also appreciate antique furniture which is hand-made out of wood. I love learning new things especially about psychology, nutrition and biology. My favorite place I have visited is Niagara Falls. It is the reason why I love butterflies and waterfalls up to this day. My favorite color is blue. It is the color of the sky and the sea. It makes me feel good spiritually and it looks good on me. I like fashion, art and rock music. I like to create my own trends. When I am not busy writing, I like watching '60's tv shows, hockey and basketball.

Thank you to our Sponsors

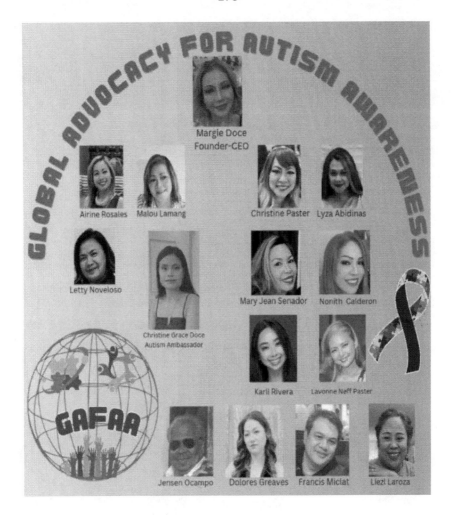

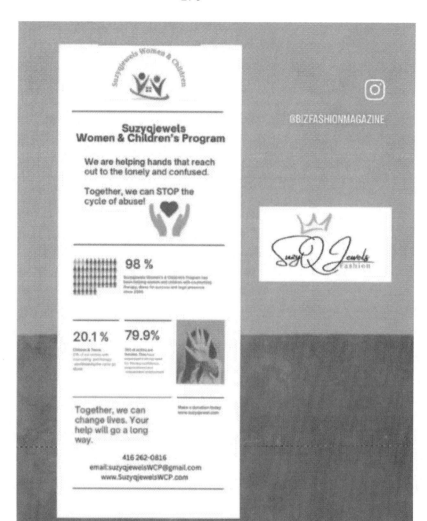

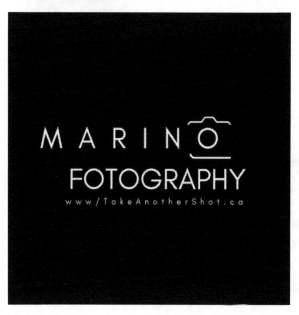

Live Your Best ME" MEonline.ca Susan Forsyth 289-675-6700
Susan.mebiz@gmail.com

181

Rsatrang and Omni TV brought Shuchi for an interview

GSAW Guest speaker Fashion show with the cycle of abuse

Manufactured by Amazon.ca
Bolton, ON

38004191R00101